Project Economic and Financial Evaluation

Applied CQRM Book Series

Volume III

Applying Monte Carlo Risk Simulation, Strategic Real Options, Stochastic Forecasting, Portfolio Optimization, Data and Decision Analytics

IIPER Press

IIPER
Press

Johnathan Mun, Ph.D.

California, USA

ROV Project Economics Analysis Tool

For Jayden, Emma, and Penny.

In a world where risk and uncertainty abound, you are the only constants in my life.

Dedicated in loving memory of my mom.

Delight yourself in the Lord and He will give you the desires of your heart.

Psalm 37:4

PREFACE

The Applied CQRM Book Series showcases how the advanced analytics covered in the Certified in Quantitative Risk Management (CQRM) certification program can be applied to real-life business problems. In Volume III, we show how ROV's PEAT software can be used to evaluate a project's economics, simulate its uncertainties, run sensitivity analysis, and use their analytical properties for making strategic decisions.

Pragmatic applications are emphasized in order to demystify the many elements inherent in risk analysis. A black box will remain a black box if no one can understand the concepts despite its power and applicability. It is only when the black box methods become transparent, so that researchers can understand, apply, and convince others of their results, value-add, and applicability, that the approaches will receive widespread attention. This transparency is achieved through step-by-step applications of quantitative modeling as well as presenting multiple cases and discussing real-life applications.

This book is targeted at those individuals who have completed the CQRM certification program but can also be used by anyone familiar with basic quantitative research methods—there is something for everyone. It is also applicable for use as a second-year MBA/MS-level or introductory PhD textbook. The examples in the book assume some prior knowledge of the subject matter.

Additional information on the CQRM program can be obtained at:

www.iiper.org

www.realoptionsvaluation.com

www.rovusa.com

v

Dr. Johnathan C. Mun is the founder, chairman, and CEO of Real Options Valuation, Inc. (ROV), a consulting, training, and software development firm specializing in strategic real options, financial valuation, Monte Carlo risk simulation, stochastic forecasting, optimization, decision analytics, business intelligence, healthcare analytics, enterprise risk management, project risk management, quantitative research methods, and risk analysis located in northern Silicon Valley, California. ROV has partners around the world including Argentina, Beijing, Chicago, China, Colombia, Ghana, Hong Kong, India, Italy, Japan, Malaysia, Mexico City, New York, Nigeria, Peru, Puerto Rico, Russia, Saudi Arabia, Shanghai, Singapore, Slovenia, South Africa, South Korea, Spain, United Kingdom, Venezuela, Zurich, and others. ROV also has a local office in Shanghai.

Dr. Mun is also the chairman of the International Institute of Professional Education and Research (IIPER), an accredited global organization staffed by professors from named universities from around the world that provides the Certified in Quantitative Risk Management (CQRM) and Certified in Risk Management (CRM) designations, among others. He is the creator of many powerful software tools including Risk Simulator, Real Options SLS Super Lattice Solver, Modeling Toolkit, Project Economics Analysis Tool (PEAT), Credit Market Operational Liquidity Risk (CMOL), Employee Stock Options Valuation, ROV BizStats, ROV Modeler Suite (Basel Credit Modeler, Risk Modeler, Optimizer, and Valuator), ROV Compiler, ROV Extractor and Evaluator, ROV Dashboard, ROV Quantitative Data Miner, and other software applications, as well as the risk-analysis training DVD. He holds public seminars on risk analysis and CQRM programs. He has over 21 registered patents and patents pending globally. He has authored over 23 books published by John Wiley & Sons, Elsevier Science, IIPER Press, and ROV Press, including multiple volumes of the Applied CQRM Series (IIPER Press, 2019-2020); *Modeling Risk: Applying Monte Carlo Simulation, Strategic Real Options, Stochastic Forecasting, Portfolio Optimization, Data Analytics, Business Intelligence, and Decision Modeling,* First Edition (Wiley, 2006), Second Edition (Wiley, 2010), and Third Edition

(ROV Press, 2015); *The Banker's Handbook on Credit Risk* (2008); *Advanced Analytical Models: 250 Applications from Basel II Accord to Wall Street and Beyond* (2008); *Real Options Analysis: Tools and Techniques,* First Edition (2003) and Second Edition (2005); *Real Options Analysis Course: Business Cases* (2003); *Applied Risk Analysis: Moving Beyond Uncertainty* (2003); and *Valuing Employee Stock Options* (2004). His books and software are being used at over 350 top universities around the world, including the Bern Institute in Germany, Chung-Ang University in South Korea, Georgetown University, ITESM in Mexico, Massachusetts Institute of Technology, U.S. Naval Postgraduate School, New York University, Stockholm University in Sweden, University of the Andes in Chile, University of Chile, University of Hull, University of Pennsylvania Wharton School, University of York in the United Kingdom, and Edinburgh University in Scotland, among others.

Currently a risk, finance, and economics professor, Dr. Mun has taught courses in financial management, investments, real options, economics, and statistics at the undergraduate and the graduate MS, MBA, and PhD levels. He teaches and has taught at universities all over the world, from the U.S. Naval Postgraduate School (Monterey, California) and University of Applied Sciences (Switzerland and Germany) as full professor, to Golden Gate University (California) and St. Mary's College (California), and has chaired many graduate research MBA thesis and PhD dissertation committees. He also teaches weeklong Risk Analysis, Real Options Analysis, and Risk Analysis for Managers public courses where participants can obtain the CRM and CQRM designations on completion. He is a senior fellow at the Magellan Center and sits on the board of standards at the American Academy of Financial Management.

He was formerly the Vice President of Analytics at Decisioneering, Inc., where he headed the development of options and financial analytics software products, analytical consulting, training, and technical support, and where he was the creator of the Real Options Analysis Toolkit software, the older and much less powerful predecessor of the Real Options Super Lattice software. Prior to joining Decisioneering, he was a Consulting Manager and Financial Economist in the Valuation Services and Global Financial Services practice of KPMG Consulting and a Manager with the Economic Consulting Services practice at KPMG LLP.

He has extensive experience in econometric modeling, financial analysis, real options, economic analysis, and statistics. During his tenure at Real Options Valuation, Inc., Decisioneering, and KPMG Consulting, he taught and consulted on a variety of real options, risk analysis, financial forecasting, project management, and financial valuation issues for more than 100 multinational firms (current and former clients include 3M, Airbus, Boeing, BP, Chevron Texaco, Financial Accounting Standards Board, Fujitsu, GE, Goodyear, Microsoft, Motorola, Northrop Grumman, Pfizer, Timken, U.S. Department of Defense, U.S. Navy, Veritas, and many others). His experience prior to joining KPMG included being department head of financial planning and analysis at Viking Inc. of FedEx, performing financial forecasting, economic analysis, and market research. Prior to that, he did financial planning and freelance financial consulting work.

Dr. Mun received a PhD in finance and economics from Lehigh University, where his research and academic interests were in the areas of investment finance, econometric modeling, financial options, corporate finance, and microeconomic theory. He also has an MBA in business administration, an MS in management science, and a BS in biology and physics. He is Certified in Financial Risk Management, Certified in Financial Consulting, and Certified in Quantitative Risk Management. He is a member of the American Mensa, Phi Beta Kappa Honor Society, and Golden Key Honor Society as well as several other professional organizations, including the Eastern and Southern Finance Associations, American Economic Association, and Global Association of Risk Professionals.

In addition, he has written many academic articles published in the *Journal of Expert Systems with Applications; Defense Acquisition Research Journal; American Institute of Physics Proceedings; Acquisitions Research (U.S. Department of Defense); Journal of the Advances in Quantitative Accounting and Finance; Global Finance Journal; International Financial Review; Journal of Financial Analysis; Journal of Applied Financial Economics; Journal of International Financial Markets, Institutions and Money; Financial Engineering News;* and *Journal of the Society of Petroleum Engineers.* Finally, he has contributed chapters in dozens of books and written over a hundred technical whitepapers, newsletters, case studies, and research papers for Real Options Valuation, Inc.

JohnathanMun@cs.com

San Francisco, California

ACCOLADES FOR DR. MUN'S BOOKS

...powerful toolset for portfolio/program managers to make rational choices among alternatives...
> Rear Admiral James Greene (Ret.), Acquisitions Chair
> Naval Postgraduate School (USA)

...unavoidable for any professional...logical, concrete, and conclusive approach...
> Jean Louis Vaysse, Vice President, Airbus (France)

...proven, revolutionary approach to quantifying risks and opportunities in an uncertain world...
> Mike Twyman, President, Mission Solutions,
> Cubic Global Defense, Inc. (USA)

...must read for anyone running investment economics...best way to quantify risk and strategic options...
> Mubarak A. Alkhater, Executive Director, New Business,
> Saudi Electric Co. (Saudi Arabia)

... pragmatic powerful risk techniques, valuable theoretical insights and analytics useful in any industry...
> Dr. Robert S. Finocchiaro, Director,
> Corporate R&D Services, 3M (USA)

...most important risk tools in one volume, definitive source on risk management with vivid examples...
> Dr. Ricardo Valerdi, Engineering Systems,
> Massachusetts Institute of Technology (USA)

...step-by-step complex concepts with unmatched ease and clarity... a "must read" for all professionals...
> Dr. Hans Weber, Product Development Leader,
> Syngenta AG (Switzerland)

...clear step-by-step approach...latest technology in decision making for real-world business...
> Dr. Paul W. Finnegan, Vice President, Alexion Pharmaceuticals (USA)

...clear roadmap and breadth of topics to create dynamic risk-adjusted strategies and options...
> Jeffrey A. Clark, Vice President Strategic Planning,
> The Timken Company (USA)

…clearly organized and tool-supported exploration of real-life business risks, options, strategy…

> Robert Mack, Vice President, Distinguished Analyst,
> Gartner Group (USA)

…full range of methodologies for quantifying and mitigating risk for effective enterprise management…

> Raymond Heika, Director of Strategic Planning,
> Northrop Grumman Corporation (USA)

…a must-read for product portfolio managers…captures risk exposure of strategic investments…

> Rafael Gutierrez, Executive Director Strategic Marketing Planning,
> Seagate Technologies (USA)

…complex topics exceptionally explained…
can understand and practice…

> Agustín Velázquez, Senior Economist,
> Venezuela Central Bank (Venezuela)

…constant source of practical applications with risk management theory…simply excellent!

> Alfredo Roisenzvit, Executive Director/Professor,
> Risk-Business Latin America (Argentina)

…the best risk modeling book is now better…
required reading by all executives…

> David Mercier, Vice President Corporate Dev.,
> Bonanza Creek Energy [Oil & Gas] (USA)

…bridge of theory and practice, intuitive, understandable interpretations…

> Luis Melo, Senior Econometrician,
> Colombia Central Bank (Colombia)

…valuable tools for corporations to deliver value to shareholders and society even in rough times…

> Dr. Markus Götz Junginger, Lead Partner,
> Gallup (Germany)

CONTENTS

PROJECT VALUATION

All companies have projects with differing sizes, investment requirements, returns, risks, strategic, and tactical value. This current book is part of the Applied CQRM series and covers the valuation of said projects or programs using economic and financial analysis methods. Advanced analytical techniques and methodologies are then added into the mix, including running scenario and sensitivity analysis, Monte Carlo risk simulation, predictive forecasting, and portfolio optimization with optimal project selection, subject to risk, budget, schedule and other constraints.

The Project Economics Analysis Tool (PEAT) software is used to illustrate how various project economics and financial results, including Net Present Value (NPV), Internal Rate of Return (IRR), Modified Internal Rate of Return (MIRR), Profitability Index (PI), Return on Investment (ROI), Payback Period (PP), and Discounted Payback Period (DPP), can be computed.

This chapter describes the main techniques (NPV, IRR, MIRR, PI, ROI, PP, and DPP) that are used in capital budgeting analysis. Each approach provides a different piece of information, so in this age of computers, managers often look at all of them when evaluating projects. However, NPV is the best single measure, and almost all firms now use NPV. The key concepts for the main techniques covered are listed below:

- Capital budgeting is the process of analyzing potential projects. Capital budgeting decisions are probably the most important ones that managers must make. Such decisions include whether a company should replace worn out/damaged equipment or replace or add to existing equipment to reduce cost; undergo expansion; or invest in a new project or equipment. At its most general, the capital budgeting process involves simply choosing the best project from among several alternatives.

- Once a potential capital budgeting project is identified, its evaluation usually requires the determination of project investment cost, project cash flow estimation, riskiness of the project, and cost of capital adjusting for riskiness of the project, as well as a determination of the key economic indicators.

- The *payback period* is defined as the number of years required to recover a project's cost. The regular *payback period method* ignores cash flows beyond the payback period, and it does not consider the time value of money. The payback does, however, provide an indication of a project's risk and liquidity, because it shows how long the invested capital will be "at risk."

- The *discounted payback* method is similar to the regular payback method except that it discounts cash flows at the project's cost of capital. It considers the time value of money, but it ignores cash flows beyond the payback period.

- The *net present value* (NPV) method discounts all cash flows at the project's cost of capital and then sums those cash flows. The project should be accepted if the NPV is positive.

- The *internal rate of return* (IRR) is defined as the discount rate that forces a project's NPV to equal zero. The project should be accepted if the IRR is greater than the cost of capital.

- The NPV and IRR methods make the same accept/reject decisions for independent projects, but if projects are mutually exclusive, ranking conflicts can arise. If conflicts arise, the NPV method should be used. The NPV and IRR methods are both superior to the payback method, but NPV is superior to IRR.

- The NPV method assumes that cash flows will be reinvested at the firm's cost of capital, while the IRR method assumes reinvestment at the project's IRR. Reinvestment at the cost of capital is a better assumption and is closer to reality.

- The *modified IRR* (MIRR) method corrects some of the problems with the regular IRR. MIRR involves finding the terminal value (TV) of the cash inflows, compounded at the firm's cost of capital, and then determining the discount rate that forces the present value of the TV to equal the present value of the outflows.

- The *profitability index* (PI) shows the dollars of present value divided by the initial cost, so this index measures relative profitability.

- Sophisticated managers consider all of the project evaluation measures because each measure provides a useful piece of information.

- Payback measures liquidity, NPV measures direct dollar benefit, IRR measures percentage return with a safety margin built in, MIRR measures a percentage return considering a better reinvestment rate, and PI measures bang for the buck.

- The post-audit is a key element of capital budgeting. By comparing actual results with predicted results and then determining why differences occurred, decision makers can improve both their operations and their forecasts of projects' outcomes.

- Small firms tend to use the payback method rather than a discounted cash flow method. This may be rational because (1) the cost of conducting a Discounted Cash Flow analysis may outweigh the benefits for the project being considered, (2) the firm's cost of capital cannot be estimated accurately, or (3) the small-business owner may be considering non-monetary goals.

- If mutually exclusive projects have unequal lives, it may be necessary to adjust the analysis to put the projects on an equal-life basis. This can be done using the replacement chain (common life) approach.

- A project's true value may be greater than the NPV based on its physical life if it can be terminated at the end of its economic life.

- Flotation costs and increased riskiness associated with unusually large expansion programs can cause the marginal cost of capital to rise as the size of the capital budget increases.

- Capital rationing occurs when management places a constraint on the size of the firm's capital budget during a particular period.

NET PRESENT VALUE

The net present value (NPV) method is simple and powerful: *All future cash flows are discounted at the project's cost of capital and then summed.* Be aware that cash flow at time zero (CF_0) is usually a negative number as this may be an initial capital investment in the project. Complications include differing life spans and different rankings using IRR. The general rule is if NPV > 0, accept the project; if NPV < 0, reject the project; if NPV = 0, you are indifferent (other qualitative variables need to be considered). The NPV is the sum of cash flows (CF) from time zero ($t = 0$) to the final cash flow period (N) discounted as some discount rate (k), which is typically the weighted average cost of capital (WACC):

$$NPV = CF_0 + \frac{CF_1}{(1+k)^1} + \frac{CF_2}{(1+k)^2} + \ldots + \frac{CF_N}{(1+k)^N} = \sum_{t=0}^{N} \frac{CF_t}{(1+k)^t}$$

$$NPV = CF_0 + \frac{CF_1}{(1+WACC)^1} + \frac{CF_2}{(1+WACC)^2} + \ldots + \frac{CF_N}{(1+WACC)^N}$$
$$= \sum_{t=0}^{N} \frac{CF_t}{(1+WACC)^t}$$

NPV has a direct relationship between economic value added (EVA) and market value added (MVA). It is equal to the present value of the project's future EVA, and, hence, a positive NPV usually implies a positive EVA and MVA.

INTERNAL RATE OF RETURN

Internal rate of return (IRR) is the discount rate that equates the project's cost to the sum of the present cash flow of the project. That is, setting NPV = 0 and solving for k in the NPV equation, where k is now called *IRR*. In other words, where:

$$NPV = \sum_{t=0}^{N} \frac{CF_t}{(1 + IRR)^t} = 0$$

Note that there may exist multiple IRRs when the cash flow stream is erratic. Also, the IRR and NPV rankings may be dissimilar. The general rule is that when IRR > required rate of return or hurdle rate or cost of capital, accept the project. That is, if the IRR exceeds the cost of capital required to finance and pay for the project, a surplus remains after paying for the project, which is passed on to the shareholders. The NPV and IRR methods make the same accept/reject decisions for *independent* projects, but if projects are *mutually exclusive*, ranking conflicts can arise. If conflicts arise, the NPV method should be used. (The NPV and IRR methods are both superior to the payback, but NPV is superior to IRR.) Conflicts may arise when the cash flow timing (most of the cash flows come in during the early years compared to later years in another project) and amounts (the cost of one project is significantly larger than another) are vastly different from one project to another. Finally, there sometimes can arise *multiple* IRR solutions in erratic cash flow streams such as large cash outflows occurring during or at the end of a project's life. In such situations, the NPV provides a more robust and accurate assessment of the project's value.

MODIFIED INTERNAL RATE OF RETURN

The NPV method assumes that the project cash flows are reinvested at the cost of capital, whereas the IRR method assumes project cash flows are reinvested at the project's own IRR. The reinvestment rate at the cost of capital is the more correct approach in that this is the firm's opportunity cost of money (if funds were not available, then capital is raised at this cost).

The modified internal rate of return (MIRR) method is intended to overcome two IRR shortcomings by setting the cash flows to be reinvested at the cost of capital and not its own IRR, as well as preventing the occurrence of multiple IRRs, because only a single MIRR will exist for all cash flow scenarios. Also, NPV and MIRR will usually result in the same project selection when projects are of equal size (significant scale differences might still result in a conflict between MIRR and NPV ranking).

The MIRR is the discount rate that forces the present value of costs of cash outflows (COF) to be equal to the present value of the terminal value (the future value of cash inflows, or CIF, compounded at the project's cost of capital, k).

$$\sum_{t=0}^{n} \frac{COF_t}{(1+k)^t} = \sum_{t=0}^{n} \frac{CIF_t(1+k)^{n-t}}{(1+MIRR)^n}$$

$$\sum_{t=0}^{n} \frac{COF_t}{(1+WACC)^t} = \sum_{t=0}^{n} \frac{CIF_t(1+WACC)^{n-t}}{(1+MIRR)^n}$$

$$PV\ Costs = \frac{Terminal\ Value}{(1+MIRR)^n}$$

PROFITABILITY INDEX

The profitability index (PI) is the ratio of the sum of the present value of cash flows to the initial cost of the project, which measures its *relative profitability*. A project is acceptable if PI > 1, and the higher the PI, the higher the project ranks. PI is mathematically very similar to return on investment (ROI). PI is a relative measure whereas ROI is an absolute measure. It returns a ratio *(the ratio is an absolute value, ignoring the negative investment cost)* while ROI is usually described as a percentage.

$$PI = \frac{\sum_{t=1}^{n} \frac{CF_t}{(1+k)^t}}{CF_0} = \frac{Benefit}{Cost} = \frac{PV\ Cash\ Flows}{Initial\ Cost}$$

$$ROI = \frac{\sum_{t=1}^{n} \frac{CF_t}{(1+k)^t} - CF_0}{CF_0} = \frac{Benefit - Cost}{Cost} = PI - 1$$

Mathematically, NPV, IRR, MIRR, and PI should provide similar rankings although conflicts may sometimes arise, and all methods should be considered as each provides a different set of relevant information.

PAYBACK PERIOD

Simple but ineffective by itself, the payback period (PP) method calculates the time necessary to pay back the initial cost (i.e., a break-even analysis). It does not take into account time valuation of money, and it does not consider different life spans after the initial payback breakpoint and ignores the cost of capital. The payback period approach helps identify the project's *liquidity* in determining how long funds will be tied up in the project.

$$Payback = Year\ before\ full\ recovery + [unrecovered\ cost \div Cash\ Flow\ at\ time\ t]$$

DISCOUNTED PAYBACK PERIOD

The discounted payback period (DPP) method is similar to the payback period method, but the cash flows used are in present values. This solves the issue of cost of capital, but the disadvantage of ignoring cash flows beyond the payback period still remains.

$$Discounted\ Payback = Year\ before\ full\ recovery + [unrecovered\ cost \div PV\ Cash\ Flow\ at\ time\ t]$$

EXAMPLE COMPUTATIONS

Payback Period (PP)

Suppose you are to choose between two projects, A and B. Project A costs $442 but pays back $200 for the next 3 years, while B costs $718 and pays back $250, $575, and $100 for the next 3 years.

The manual calculations are show below and in Figure 1.1.

Payback A is between years 2 and 3, as
$$- \$442\ pays\ back\ between\ \$200$$
$$+ \$200\ in\ year\ 2\ and\ \$200 + \$200 + \$200\ in\ year\ 3$$

2 years is $200 + $200 or $400 paid back, with $442 − $400
$$= \$42\ remaining\ to\ be\ paid\ back\ in\ year\ 3$$

$$Payback\ A = 2 + [\$42 \div \$200] = 2.21\ years$$

Payback B is between years 1 and 2, as
$$- \$718\ pays\ back\ between\ \$250\ in\ year\ 1\ and\ \$250$$
$$+ \$575\ in\ year\ 2$$

1 year is $250 paid back, with $718
$$- \$250\ remaining\ to\ be\ paid\ back\ in\ year\ 2$$

$$Payback\ B = 1 + [(\$718 - \$250) \div \$575] = 1.81\ years$$

PAYBACK PERIOD

Suppose you are to choose between two projects, A and B. Project A costs $442 but pays back $200 for the next 3 years while Project B costs $718 and pays back $250, $575 and $100 for the next 3 years:

Project A:

Time	0	1	2	3
Cash Flow	($442)	$200	$200	$200

Project B:

Time	0	1	2	3
Cash Flow	($718)	$250	$575	$100

We compute the cumulative positive cash flow and find the year prior to payback, and then add the proportion of unpaid balance to the cash flow of the following year:

Project A:

Time	0	1	2	3
Cash Flow	($442)	$200	$200	$200
CUM +CF		$200	$400	$600

Year prior to payback:	2
Unpaid Amount:	($42)
Proportion of Following Year:	0.21
Payback Period (Years):	**2.21**

Project B:

Time	0	1	2	3
Cash Flow	($718)	$250	$575	$100
CUM +CF		$250	$825	$925

Year prior to payback:	1
Unpaid Amount:	($468)
Proportion of Following Year:	0.81
Payback Period (Years):	**1.81**

Figure 1.1: Payback Period Manual Computations

- *Neglects time value of money.* To solve this, use present values instead of cash flows, that is, use a discounted payback period instead. This means that in the example above, the $200, or $250, $575, and $100 cash flows are first discounted to present values. See the Discounted Payback Period example below.

- *Cash flows and length of time remaining are left out after the payback period.* As an example, suppose we have two new projects, X and Y with cash flows as shown below. Both have identical payback periods but clearly, project Y is superior as it has additional cash flows. These cash flows post payback period are ignored.

Project X

$t=0$	1	2	3
-100	100	100	100

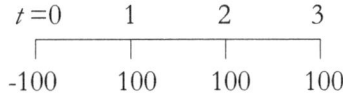

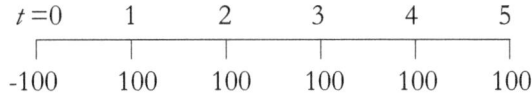

Payback = 1 year

Project Y

$t=0$	1	2	3	4	5
-100	100	100	100	100	100

Payback = 1 year

Discounted Payback Period (DPP)

Suppose you are to choose between two projects, A and B. Project A costs $442 but pays back $200 for the next 3 years, while B costs $718 and pays back $250, $575, and $100 for the next 3 years. Further suppose that the WACC discount rate is 12%. The manual computations are shown below and in Figure 1.2.

$Discounted\ Payback\ A\ =\ 2\ +\ [(\$442 - \$338.0) \div \$142.4]$
$=\ 2.73\ years$

$Discounted\ Payback\ B\ =\ 2\ +\ [(\$718 - \$681.6) \div \$71.2]\ =\ 2.51\ years$

DISCOUNTED PAYBACK PERIOD

Suppose you are to choose between two projects, A and B. Project A costs $442 but pays back $200 for the next 3 years while Project B costs $718 and pays back $250, $575 and $100 for the next 3 years. Now suppose the WACC discount rate is 12%.

Project A:

Time	0	1	2	3
Cash Flow	($442)	$200	$200	$200

Project B:

Time	0	1	2	3
Cash Flow	($718)	$250	$575	$100

We compute the cumulative positive cash flow and find the year prior to payback, and then add the proportion of unpaid balance to the cash flow of the following year:

Project A:

Time	0	1	2	3
Cash Flow	($442)	$200	$200	$200
PV Cash Flow	($442)	$178.6	$159.4	$142.4
CUM +CF		$178.6	$338.0	$480.4

Year prior to payback:	2
Unpaid Amount:	($104)
Proportion of Following Year:	0.73
Payback Period (Years):	**2.73**

Project B:

Time	0	1	2	3
Cash Flow	($718)	$250	$575	$100
PV Cash Flow	($718)	$223.2	$458.4	$71.2
CUM +CF		$223.2	$681.6	$752.8

Year prior to payback:	2
Unpaid Amount:	($36)
Proportion of Following Year:	0.51
Payback Period (Years):	**2.51**

Figure 1.2: Discounted Payback Period Manual Computations

Using the projects A and B below, which project is better assuming a 12% WACC discount rate? Use the NPV method.

Project A

$t=0$	1	2	3
-442	200	200	200

Project B

$t=0$	1	2	3
-718	250	575	100

$$NPV = CF_0 + \frac{CF_1}{(1+k)^1} + \frac{CF_2}{(1+k)^2} + \cdots + \frac{CF_N}{(1+k)^N} = \sum_{t=0}^{N} \frac{CF_t}{(1+k)^t}$$

$$NPV_A = -\$442 + \frac{\$200}{(1+0.12)^1} + \frac{\$200}{(1+0.12)^2} + \frac{\$200}{(1+0.12)^3}$$

$$NPV_A = -\$442 + \$178.6 + \$159.4 + \$142.4 = \$38.37$$

$$NPV_B = -\$718 + \frac{\$250}{(1+0.12)^1} + \frac{\$575}{(1+0.12)^2} + \frac{\$100}{(1+0.12)^3}$$

$$NPV_A = -\$718 + \$223.2 + \$458.4 + \$71.2 = \$34.78$$

Comparing A and B, A has a higher NPV, therefore A should be chosen before B although both projects should be undertaken if there exist sufficient funds, otherwise, only undertake project A. Rank remains the same but NPV values differ using different discount rates. Figure 1.3 shows the computations in Excel using the NPV function. Please note that Excel's NPV function starts from Year 1, which means you need to set the function for cash flows from Years 1 to N, and add the cash flow of Year 0, as illustrated in Figure 1.3's two NPV functions.

NET PRESENT VALUE (NPV)

Suppose you are to choose between two projects, A and B. Project A costs $442 but pays back $200 for the next 3 years while Project B costs $718 and pays back $250, $575 and $100 for the next 3 years. Now suppose the WACC discount rate is 12%.

Project A:

Time	0	1	2	3
Cash Flow	($442)	$200	$200	$200

Project B:

Time	0	1	2	3
Cash Flow	($718)	$250	$575	$100

Manually:: We compute the Present Value (PV) of the Cash Flows (CF) and sum them to obtain the Net Present Value (NPV):

Project A:

Time	0	1	2	3
Cash Flow	($442)	$200	$200	$200
PVCF	($442.0)	$178.6	$159.4	$142.4
SUM (NPV)	$38.37			

Project B:

Time	0	1	2	3
Cash Flow	($718)	$250	$575	$100
PV Cash Flow	($718.0)	$223.2	$458.4	$71.2
SUM (NPV)	$34.78			

Using Excel's NPV Function:

NPV	$38.37	<<=NPV(12%,E14:G14)+D14>>

NPV	$34.78	<<=NPV(12%,L14:N14)+K14>>

* Be careful as Excel's NPV function requires the starting CF be from year 1 and not year 0, which means you need to add back CF at Year 0, otherwise you will obtain incorrect results (e.g., instead of $38.37, you get $34.26, and instead of $34.78 you get $31.05).

Figure 1.3: Net Present Value Manual Computations

Using the same scenario above, calculate the IRR for projects A and B assuming a 12% WACC discount rate (this will now be used as the hurdle rate). Should we accept both projects again, and which project is better?

$$NPV = \sum_{t=0}^{N} \frac{CF_t}{(1 + IRR)^t} = 0$$

$$NPV = CF_0 + \frac{CF_1}{(1 + IRR)^1} + \frac{CF_2}{(1 + IRR)^2} + \cdots + \frac{CF_N}{(1 + IRR)^N} = \sum_{t=0}^{N} \frac{CF_t}{(1 + IRR)^t}$$

$$-\$442 + \frac{\$200}{(1 + IRR_A)^1} + \frac{\$200}{(1 + IRR_A)^2} + \frac{\$200}{(1 + IRR_A)^3} = 0$$

$$-\$718 + \frac{\$250}{(1 + IRR_B)^1} + \frac{\$575}{(1 + IRR_B)^2} + \frac{\$100}{(1 + IRR_B)^3} = 0$$

Using trial and error, simple optimization, or search function (Goal Seek in Excel), we obtain IRR for project A to be 16.99% and 14.99% for project B. The decision should be to choose Project A over B as it has a higher return (IRR) and IRR $> k$ for both. Figure 1.4 shows the annual computations of IRR using Excel's IRR function (unlike the NPV function that starts with Year 1 cash flow, the IRR function starts with Year 0's cash flow as illustrated in the figure).

Multiple Internal Rate of Returns

When cash flows are both + and −, there may exist multiple IRRs. For instance, consider a project costing −$1.6M with returns of +$10M in the first year and a loss of −$10M in the second year. What is the project's IRR?

$$NPV = -\$1.6 + \frac{\$10}{(1 + IRR)^1} + \frac{-\$10}{(1 + IRR)^2} = 0$$

Solving yields $IRR = 25\%$ and 400%

The conclusion is that one should use all methods at one's disposal and see which makes more sense. In regular situations, they should all have similar results. Figure 1.5 shows how multiple IRR errors can exist with a simple fluctuating cash flow.

INTERNAL RATE OF RETURN (IRR)

Suppose you are to choose between two projects, A and B. Project A costs $442 but pays back $200 for the next 3 years while Project B costs $718 and pays back $250, $575 and $100 for the next 3 years. Now suppose the WACC discount rate is 12%.

Project A:

Time	0	1	2	3
Cash Flow	($442)	$200	$200	$200

Project B:

Time	0	1	2	3
Cash Flow	($718)	$250	$575	$100

Manually:: We compute the Present Value (PV) of the Cash Flows (CF) and sum them to obtain the Net Present Value (NPV), and then either perform a trial and error test of the required discount rate such that NPV = 0, or use a Goal Seek method to obtain the IRR result.

Project A:

Time	0	1	2	3
Cash Flow	($442)	$200	$200	$200
PVCF	($442.0)	$171.0	$146.1	$124.9
TEST RATE	16.99%			
SUM (NPV)	$0.00			

Project B:

Time	0	1	2	3
Cash Flow	($718)	$250	$575	$100
PV Cash Flow	($718.0)	$217.4	$434.8	$65.8
TEST RATE	14.99%			
SUM (NPV)	$0.00			

Goal Seek

Set cell: D17
To value: 0
By changing cell: D16
OK   Cancel

Goal Seek

Set cell: K17
To value: 0
By changing cell: K16
OK   Cancel

Using Excel's IRR Function:

IRR   16.99%   << =IRR(D14:G14) >>

IRR   14.99%   << =IRR(K14:N14) >>

* Be careful as Excel's NPV function requires the starting CF be from year 1 and not year 0, which means you need to add back CF at Year 0, otherwise you will obtain incorrect results (e.g. instead of $38.37, you get $34.26, and instead of $34.78 you get $31.05).

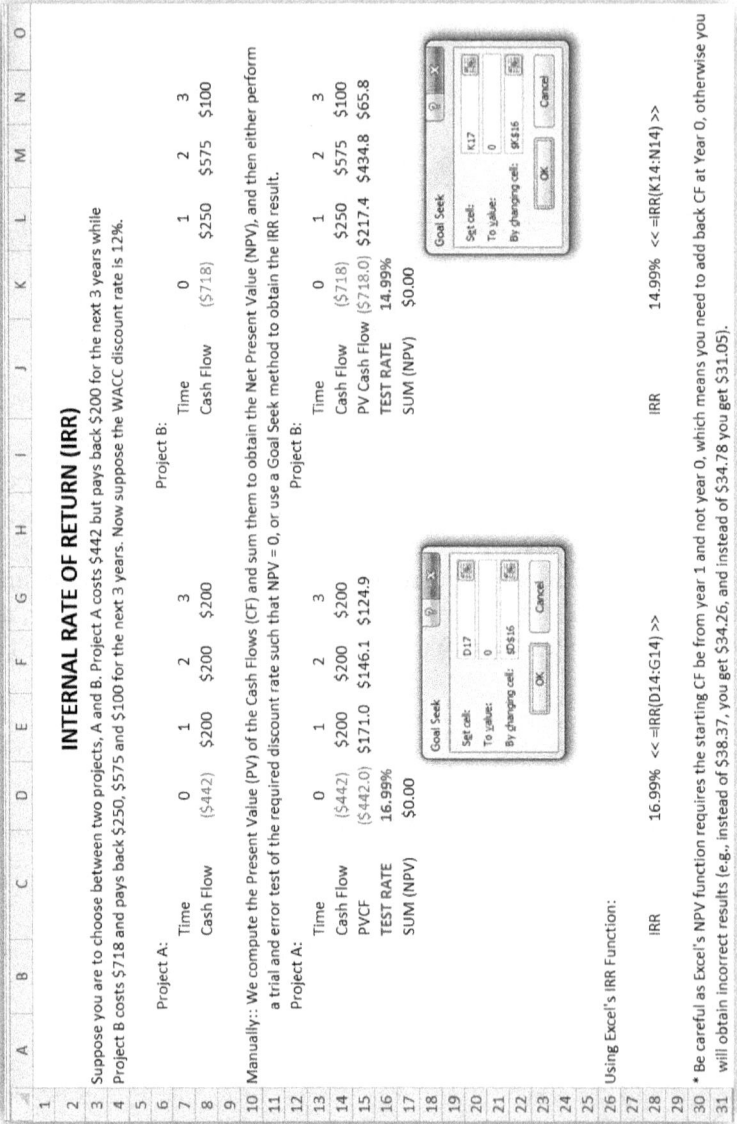

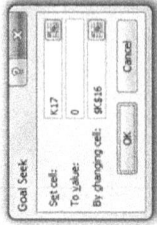

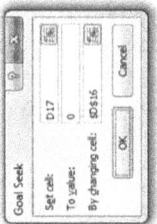

Figure 1.4: Internal Rate of Return Manual Computations

MULTIPLE IRR ERROR EXAMPLE

When cash flows are both + and –, there may exist multiple IRRs. For instance, consider a project costing –$1.6M and returns +$10M in the first year and a loss of –$10M in the second year. What is the project's IRR?

Result 1:

Time	0	1	2
Cash Flow	($1.6)	$10.0	($10.0)

Result 2:

Time	0	1	2
Cash Flow	($1.6)	$10.0	($10.0)

Manually:: We compute the Present Value (PV) of the Cash Flows (CF) and sum them to obtain the Net Present Value (NPV), and then either perform a trial and error test of the required discount rate such that NPV = 0, or use a Goal Seek method to obtain the IRR result.

Result 1:

Time	0	1	2
Cash Flow	($1.6)	$10.0	($10.0)
PVCF	($1.6)	$8.0	($6.4)
TEST RATE	25.0%		
SUM (NPV)	$0.00		

Result 2:

Time	0	1	2
Cash Flow	($1.6)	$10.0	($10.0)
PV Cash Flow	($1.6)	$2.0	($0.4)
TEST RATE	400.0%		
SUM (NPV)	$0.00		

Figure 1.5: Multiple IRR Error

Modified Internal Rate of Return (MIRR)

Calculate the MIRR for the two projects A and B as specified previously. Figure 1.6 shows the manual computations of the modified internal rate of return (MIRR) using cash out-flows (COF) and cash in-flows (CIF):

$$\sum_{t=0}^{n} \frac{COF_t}{(1 + WACC)^t} = \sum_{t=0}^{n} \frac{CIF_t(1 + WACC)^{n-t}}{(1 + MIRR)^n}$$

which is equivalent to

$$|PV\ Costs| = \frac{Terminal\ Value}{(1 + MIRR)^n}$$

$$PV\ Costs = \frac{-\$442}{(1 + 0.12)^0} = -\$442$$

$$Terminal\ Value_A = \frac{\$200}{(1 + 0.12)^2} + \frac{\$200}{(1 + 0.12)^1} + \frac{\$200}{(1 + 0.12)^0}$$

$$= \$250.9 + \$224.0 + \$200.0 = \$674.9$$

$$|PV\ Costs_A| = \frac{Terminal\ Value_A}{(1 + MIRR_A)^n} \quad means \quad \$442 = \frac{\$674.9}{(1 + MIRR)^3}$$

Solving yields MIRR = 15.15% for project A.

$$Terminal\ Value_B = \frac{\$250}{(1 + 0.12)^2} + \frac{\$575}{(1 + 0.12)^1} + \frac{\$100}{(1 + 0.12)^0}$$

$$= \$313.6 + \$644.0 + \$100.0 = \$1057.6$$

$$PV\ Costs = \frac{-\$718}{(1 + 0.12)^0} = -\$718$$

$$|PV\ Costs_A| = \frac{Terminal\ Value_A}{(1 + MIRR_A)^n} \quad means \quad \$718 = \frac{\$1057.6}{(1 + MIRR)^3}$$

Solving yields MIRR = 13.78% for project B.

Compute the profitability index (PI) and return on investment (ROI) on Projects A and B as previously specified. Figure 1.7 shows the manual computation of the PI and ROI.

$$PI = \frac{\sum_{t=1}^{n} \frac{CF_t}{(1+k)^t}}{CF_0} = \frac{Benefit}{Cost} = \frac{PV\ Cash\ Flows}{Initial\ Cost}$$

$$PI = \frac{\sum_{t=1}^{n} \frac{CF_t}{(1+k)^t}}{CF_0}$$

$$PI_A = \frac{\frac{\$200}{(1+0.12)^1} + \frac{\$200}{(1+0.12)^2} + \frac{\$200}{(1+0.12)^3}}{\frac{\$442}{(1+0.12)^0}} = \frac{\$480.4}{\$442.0} = 1.0868$$

$$ROI = \frac{\sum_{t=1}^{n} \frac{CF_t}{(1+k)^t} - CF_0}{CF_0} = \frac{Benefit - Cost}{Cost}$$

$$ROI_A = PI - 1 = 1.0868 - 1 = 8.68\%$$

$$PI_B = \frac{\frac{\$250}{(1+0.12)^1} + \frac{\$575}{(1+0.12)^2} + \frac{\$100}{(1+0.12)^3}}{\frac{\$718}{(1+0.12)^0}} = \frac{\$752.8}{\$718.0} = 1.0484$$

$$ROI_B = PI - 1 = 1.0484 - 1 = 4.84\%$$

We see that ROI and PI of project A exceeds that of project B, so we would recommend going ahead with project A instead of project B.

MODIFIED INTERNAL RATE OF RETURN (MIRR)

Suppose you are to choose between two projects, A and B. Project A costs $442 but pays back $200 for the next 3 years while Project B costs $718 and pays back $250, $575 and $100 for the next 3 years. Now suppose the WACC discount rate is 12%.

Project A:

Time	0	1	2	3
Cash Flow	($442)	$200	$200	$200

Project B:

Time	0	1	2	3
Cash Flow	($718)	$250	$575	$100

Manually:: We compute the Present Value (PV) of the Cash Flows (CF) and sum them to obtain the Net Present Value (NPV), and then either perform a trial and error test of the required discount rate such that NPV = 0, or use a Goal Seek method to obtain the IRR result.

Project A:

Time	0	1	2	3
Cash Flow	($442)	$200	$200	$200
PV (COF)	($442.0)			
FV (CIF)		$250.9	$224.0	$200.0
TV (Sum CIF)	$674.9			
PV of TV	$442.0			
TEST RATE	15.15%			
SUM (NPV)	$0.0			

Project B:

Time	0	1	2	3
Cash Flow	($718)	$250	$575	$100
PV (COF)	($718.0)			
FV (CIF)		$313.6	$644.0	$100.0
TV (Sum CIF)	$1,057.6			
PV of TV	$718.0			
TEST RATE	13.78%			
SUM (NPV)	($0.0)			

Goal Seek

Set cell: D20
To value: 0
By changing cell: D19
OK — Cancel

Goal Seek

Set cell: K20
To value: 0
By changing cell: K19
OK — Cancel

Using Excel's MIRR Function:

MIRR   15.15%   << =MIRR(D14:G14,12%,12%) >>

MIRR   13.78%   << =MIRR(K14:N14,12%,12%) >>

*The reinvestment rate is set to be the cost of capital in the MIRR method. If you set the MIRR function's reinvestment rate to be equal to the IRR, you obtain the IRR result once again. For instance, if you calculate =MIRR(D14:G14,12%,16.99%), you get 16.99%, the IRR for project A.

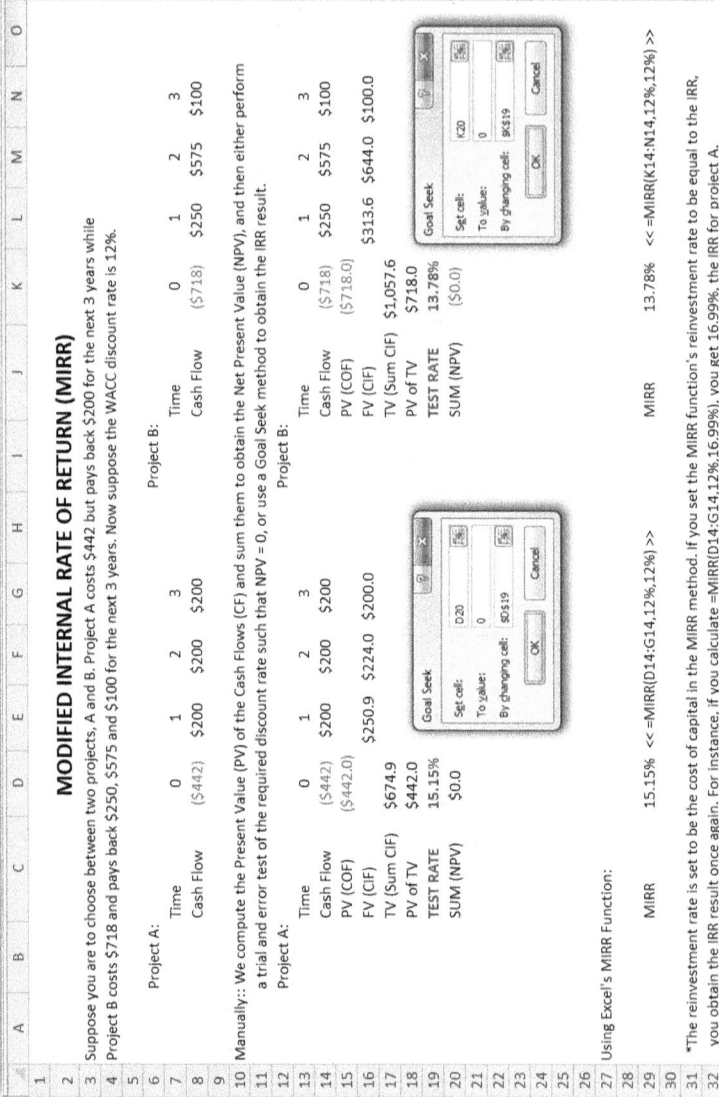

Figure 1.6: Modified Internal Rate of Return Manual Computations

PROFITABILITY INDEX (PI) AND RETURN ON INVESTMENT (ROI)

Suppose you are to choose between two projects, A and B. Project A costs $442 but pays back $200 for the next 3 years while Project B costs $718 and pays back $250, $575 and $100 for the next 3 years. Now suppose the WACC discount rate is 12%.

Project A:

Time	0	1	2	3
Cash Flow	($442)	$200	$200	$200

Project B:

Time	0	1	2	3
Cash Flow	($718)	$250	$575	$100

Manually:: We compute the Present Value (PV) of the Cash Flows (CF) for the negative CF (investment cost) and positive CF:

Project A:

Time	0	1	2	3
Cash Flow	($442)	$200	$200	$200
PVCF	($442.0)	$178.6	$159.4	$142.4
ABS(CF(0)) Cost	$442.0	<<=ABS(D15) >>		
SUM CF(i)	$480.4	<<=SUM(E15:G15) >>		

Profitability Index (PI)	1.0868	<<=D17/D16 >>
Return on Investment (ROI)	8.68%	<<=(D17-D16)/D16 >>

Project B:

Time	0	1	2	3
Cash Flow	($718)	$250	$575	$100
PV Cash Flow	($718.0)	$223.2	$458.4	$71.2
ABS(CF(0)) Cost	$718.0	<<=ABS(K15) >>		
SUM CF(i)	$752.8	<<=SUM(L15:N15) >>		

Profitability Index (PI)	1.0484	<<=K17/K16 >>
Return on Investment (ROI)	4.84%	<<=(K17-K16)/K16 >>

* We usually convert the initial investment cost (a negative value) into a positive absolute value to simplify the calculations, otherwise it is difficult to keep in mind which values are positive and which are negative. The ROI value is simply PI - 1 in percent.

Figure 1.7: Profitability Index and Return on Investment Manual Computations

PEAT SOFTWARE

Follow the steps below to get started:

1. Start the PEAT software.

2. *Select a Module* you wish to run (e.g., *Discounted Cash Flow Model*) on the main splash screen (Figure 2.1; additional modules will be added in future releases).

3. Select *Start Selected Module* (to start a new model from scratch or to open a previously saved model), or *Load Example* to load an already completed example model (this latter choice is useful when trying to learn the functionalities of the software). To follow along with the examples, select *Discounted Cash Flow* and click on *Load Example*.

The PEAT software's menu items are fairly straightforward (e.g., *File | New or File | Save*). The software is also arranged in a tabbed format. There are 3 tab-levels in the software and it is recommended that you proceed from top to bottom and left to right when performing your analysis. Complete the lowest level from left to right first before moving up a level.

Real Options Valuation

- Corporate Investments - Stochastic DCF
- Enterprise Risk Management (ERM) - Risk Register
- Project Management - Schedule and Cost Risk
- Goals Analytics - Sales and Pipeline Modeling
- Banking - Credit, Market, Operational, Liquidity Risk
- Corporate Investments - Buy vs. Lease
- Public Sector Analysis - Knowledge Value Added
- Oil and Gas Economics - Investment Decision Analysis
- Oil and Gas Economics - Oil Field Reserves
- Oil and Gas Economics - Remaining Oil Recovery
- Oil and Gas Economics - Well Type Curves
- Customized Encrypted Models

Project Economics Analysis Tool

© Copyright 2012-2017 Real Options Valuation, Inc.

Applying Integrated Risk Management methodologies (Monte Carlo risk simulation, strategic real options, stochastic forecasting, business analytics, and portfolio optimization) to project and portfolio economics and financial analysis.

| Load Example | English |
| New | Exit |

- Healthcare - Health Economics Analysis Tool (HEAT)
- Healthcare - Health Economics Analysis Tool (HEAT)
- Healthcare - Rapid Economic Justification (REJ)
- Saudi Aramco - FPD Standard Economic Model
- Saudi Aramco - FPD Expanded Economic Model
- Saudi Aramco - CFPD Standard Corporate Finance Projects
- Saudi Aramco - JV Expanded Joint Venture Valuation
- Cubic Corp - Corporate Portfolio Management
- Northrop Grumman - IR&D Model
- Northrop Grumman - S-Curve Analysis
- Multicriteria Analysis

Figure 2.1 – PEAT Splash Screen

The PEAT software has the following modules or tabs:

- **Discounted Cash Flow or Project Economics.** Depending on the module selected when the software first starts, the contents of this Level 1's tab and its subtabs will change.

- **Custom Calculations.** Allows you to enter your own custom model and calculations, and link certain cells to the other subtabs.

- **Projects.** This tab is at the heart of the software's input assumptions. You can insert, delete, edit, or reorder these Project tabs by first clicking on any Project tab and then selecting *Projects | Add, Delete, Duplicate, Rearrange,* or *Rename Project* from the menu. A Project tab is indicative of a project, an implementation path, or an alternative strategic decision. Within each Project tab, the following subtabs are available depending on the module selected:

  o **DCF: Discounted Cash Flow Model.** Revenues, expenses, capital investments, starting and ending years for the cash flow model, discount rate, and tax rates can be entered here.

  o **DCF: Cash Flow Ratios.** Additional balance sheet data can be entered (e.g., current asset, shares outstanding, common equity, total debt, etc.) and the relevant financial ratios will be computed (EBIT, Net Income, Net Cash Flow, Operating Cash Flow, Economic Value Added, Return on Invested Capital, Net Profit Margin, etc.).

  o **DCF: Economic Results.** This tab returns the computed economic and financial indicators such as Net Present Value (NPV), Internal Rate of Return (IRR), Modified Internal Rate of Return (MIRR), Profitability Index (PI), Return on Investment (ROI), Payback Period (PP), and Discounted Payback (DPP). It also features a dynamic chart where you can view the NPV Profile (calculated NPV values depending on different discount rates), time-series of cash flows for the Project, and other calculated financial metrics.

- o **DCF: Information and Details.** Here you can enter information and notes for the Project.

- o **O&G: Input Assumptions.** Revenues, expenses, capital investments, starting and ending years for the cash flow model, discount rate, and tax rates can be entered here.

- **Portfolio Analysis.** This tab returns the computed economic and financial indicators such as NPV, IRR, MIRR, PI, ROI, PP, and DPP for all the Projects combined into a portfolio view. The Economic Results (Level 3) subtabs show the individual Project's economic and financial indicators, whereas this Level 2 Portfolio Analysis view shows the results of all Projects' indicators and compares them side by side. There are also two charts available for comparing these individual Projects' results.

  - o **Applied Analytics.** This section allows you to run Tornado Analysis and Scenario Analysis on any one of the Projects previously modeled—this analytics tab is on Level 1, which means it covers all of the various Projects on Level 2. You can therefore run Tornado or Scenario on any one of the Projects.

    - ▪ **Static Tornado.** Tornado Analysis is a static sensitivity analysis of the selected model's output to each input assumption, performed one at a time, and ranked from most impactful to the least. This analysis tests all precedent variables in the model independently.

    - ▪ **Scenario Analysis.** Scenario Analysis is also a static sensitivity model that can be easily performed through a two-step process: set up the model and run the model. This analysis tests one or two variables through a range of scenarios to determine the outcome of the selected output.

      - • **Scenario Input Settings.** This is where you would set up the variables to test and specify their ranges or scenarios.

- **Scenario Output Tables.** This is where you would run the saved scenarios and obtain color-coded scenario tables ("sweetspots" and "hotspots").

o **Risk Simulation.** Set up and run Monte Carlo risk simulations on any of your Projects. Specifically, you can set up probability distribution assumptions on any combinations of inputs, run a risk simulation tens of thousands of trials, and retrieve the simulated forecast outputs as charts, statistics, probabilities, and confidence intervals in order to develop comprehensive risk profiles of the Projects.

- **Set Input Assumptions.** Start the simulation analysis by first setting simulation distributional inputs here.

- **Simulation Results.** Shows the simulated forecast charts (PDF/CDF), simulation risk statistics, percentiles, probabilities, and confidence intervals of your simulation.

- **Overlay Results.** Multiple simulation output variables can be compared at once using the Overlay Results tab.

- **Analysis of Alternatives.** This subtab shows the results of the simulation statistics in a table format as well as a chart of the statistics such that one Project can be compared against another.

- **Dynamic Sensitivity.** After a simulation is run, this is where a dynamic sensitivity analysis is performed.

o **Options Strategies.** This is where you can draw your own custom strategic map or strategic real options paths. This section only allows you to draw and visualize these strategic pathways and does not perform any computations. The next section, Options Valuation, actually performs the computations.

o **Options Valuation.** This tab performs the calculations of Real Options Valuation models.

- **Options Valuation.** Here is where you start by choosing and setting up the real options model to compute.

- **Strategy View.** Provides a visual example of the selected real option.

- **Sensitivity.** Runs a static sensitivity table of the real options model.

- **Tornado.** Develops the Tornado chart of the real options model.

- **Scenario.** Runs a scenario table of the real options model.

o **Forecast Prediction.** This is a sophisticated Business Analytics and Business Statistics module with over 150 functionalities.

- **Dataset.** Enter and edit your data here.

- **Visualize.** You can chart any data variable you have entered.

- **Command.** Provides an alternative and quicker way of executing models in the Forecast Prediction module.

- **Analysis.** Set up the analytical models (choose the model, provide it with the relevant data variables, and set the model parameters).

- **Results.** Shows the results of the analytical model, if applicable.

- **Charts.** Charts the results of the analytical model, if applicable.

- **Statistics.** Returns the statistics of the analytical model, if applicable.

o **Portfolio Optimization.** In the Portfolio Optimization section, the individual Projects can be modeled as a portfolio and optimized to determine the best combination of projects for the portfolio.

- **Optimization Settings.** Start the analysis by setting up the portfolio's objective, decision variables, and constraints here.

- **Optimization Results.** This tab returns the results from the portfolio optimization process.

- **Advanced Custom Optimization.** In this tab, you can create and solve your own customized optimization models.

o **Knowledge Center.** To assist you in quickly getting up to speed in using the software, here you will find quick getting started guides and sample procedures that are straight to the point.

- **Step by Step Procedures.** Here you will find some quick self-paced lessons on how to use PEAT.

- **Basic Project Economics Lessons.** This section provides an overview tour of some common concepts involved with cash flow analysis and project economic analysis such as the computations of NPV, IRR, MIRR, PI, ROI, PP, and DPP, as well as the basics of interpreting PDF/CDF simulation forecast charts.

o **Getting Started Videos.** Here you can watch a short description and hands-on examples of how to run one of the sections within this PEAT software.

o **Importing and Uploaded Data.** There is a *File | Import Data* menu function to upload specific Excel files. Locate the sample templates from the installation folder of PEAT (e.g., C:\Program Files (x86)\Real Options Valuation\ROV PEAT) and locate the two template versions, *"DCF Upload Template.xlsx"* and *"DCF Upload Template with Automation.xlsx"*. The first file has a simple upload template for 12 years and 6 revenue and cost categories, which is sufficient in most cases. This file has a wide area on the right for additional scratch work as needed. The second file has additional automation and allows up to 10 revenue and cost categories as well as up to 50 years of cash flows, but limited areas on the right for additional scratch work. Regardless of the file used, note the following:

- Not all rows need to be populated. In the appropriate rows, enter the relevant information in the cells with borders. Note that there are error checks for the data inputs, where $Min \leq Likely \leq Max$ is required.

- Only worksheets with the prefix *"DCF"* will be imported into PEAT; other worksheets without this prefix will not be uploaded. This allows you to have additional intermediate calculation worksheets stored in this same workbook that will not be uploaded into PEAT.

- The *Short Project Name* (cell B5) will become the name of the project tab in PEAT. Make sure this is a unique, short, simple but descriptive name, otherwise the import function will not work correctly. Proceed to enter the *Starting Year* and *Ending Year*, where Starting Year < Ending Year. Note that the starting year is the base year to which the discounting will be set as the present value year. Complete the preliminary data input with the range of discount rates and marginal tax rates (the discount and tax rates can be static without setting a range). The template will automatically add the relevant columns based on the ending year entered.

- For each row of revenues, costs, and investments, enter the line item names (column B) and proceed to enter the minimum, most likely, and maximum values for each year. If there are unused rows, leave those sections completely empty. When done, do a *save as* to create a new file name and exit Microsoft Excel.

- To execute the data import, start PEAT and select *Corporate Investments – Stochastic DCF*. Then, click on *File | Import Data* and browse to this saved Excel file. After the import is successful, remember to save the PEAT file. Then, proceed to run the models as usual.

- Note that the import function currently supports only triangular distributions, hence, the minimum, likely, and maximum inputs. These simulation assumptions will be automatically imported into PEAT's simulation assumptions tab, with a default of 10,000 trials and a seed value of 123. Clearly, these can be changed as required.

- When adding additional projects, just duplicate the "DCF" worksheets as appropriate. Remember to delete unneeded DCF worksheets otherwise empty projects will be imported. Alternatively, rename the worksheet to not include the three letters, DCF, so that these worksheets will not be automatically uploaded.

- Do not make any modifications to the structure of the template such as adding or deleting rows and columns or changing the headers and titles. Making these modifications will invalidate the template and the data import will not run correctly.

PROJECT ECONOMICS USING PEAT

The *Project Economics* section is the heart of your input assumptions. Here you would enter your input assumptions, set up the project economics model, identify and create the various Projects, and compute the economic and financial results such as Net Present Value (NPV), Internal Rate of Return (IRR), Modified Internal Rate of Return (MIRR), Profitability Index (PI), Return on Investment (ROI), Payback Period (PP), and Discounted Payback (DPP). This section will also auto generate various charts, cash flow models, intermediate calculations, and comparisons of your Projects within a portfolio view.

Project | Discounted Cash Flow

When in any of the Project tabs, the *Projects* menu will become available, ready for you to add, delete, duplicate, or rename a Project or rearrange the order of the Projects tabs by first clicking on any Projects tab and then selecting *Projects | Add, Delete, Duplicate, Rearrange,* or *Rename Project* from the menu. All of the required functionalities such as input assumptions, adding or reducing the number of rows, selecting discount rate type, or copying the grid are available within each Project tab.

The input assumptions you enter in these Project tabs are localized and used only within each tab. When setting up your model in the Project tab (Level 2), proceed from left to right of the Level 3 subtabs. Required input assumptions are shown as input boxes (e.g., seen as white input boxes in Figure 3.1) and computed results are shown as data grids. Finally, if your model is large, you can click on the *View Full Grid* for a pop-up view of the entire model.

Revenues, expenses, capital investments, starting and ending years for the cash flow model, discount rate, and tax rates can be entered here. Below are some tips on using this tab:

- Enter all the required inputs, and if certain cells are irrelevant, enter zeros. You can also select some data from Excel and right-click on any cell and paste the data for the entire row or multiple rows and columns. You can also right-click and select *Paste Absolute Values* or *Paste with Signed Reversed* if required (e.g., these are valuable if your Excel data uses negative values to represent expenses whereas PEAT requires positive values as expenses).

- You can increase or decrease the number of rows for each category as required.

- The *DCF Starting Year* input is the discounting base year, where all cash flows will be present valued to this year. Make sure to complete the starting and ending years correctly prior to entering or pasting any data into the grid. Changing starting or ending years after all the analysis is done may invalidate some of the results.

- The main categories are in boldface, and the input boxes under the categories are for you to enter in the line item name/label.

- Remember to scroll down the user interface to continue entering additional required critical inputs (e.g., *Capital Expenditures*).

- You can either apply a constant tax % rate to compute taxes or use your own custom inputs.

- You can click on *Copy Grid* to copy the results into the Windows clipboard in order to paste into another software application such as Microsoft Excel or Word.

- You can also click on the *View Full Grid* to see the entire model as a pop-up screen. This facilitates viewing of a large model and reduces the need for scrolling horizontally and vertically. It also helps when you are attempting to take a screenshot of the entire model.

Additional balance sheet data can be entered here (e.g., current asset, shares outstanding, common equity, total debt, etc.), as seen in Figure 3.2, and the relevant financial ratios will be computed (EBIT, Net Income, Net Cash Flow, Operating Cash Flow, Economic Value Added, Return on Invested Capital, Net Profit Margin, etc.). Computed results or intermediate calculations are shown as data grids. Data grid rows are color coded by alternate rows for easy viewing. As usual, you can click on *Copy Grid* to copy the computations to the Windows clipboard from which you can then paste into another software such as Microsoft Excel. Here are some tips on using the Cash Flow Ratios tab:

- Enter the input assumptions as best you can; you can guess at some of these figures to get started. The inputs entered in this *Cash Flow Ratios* subtab will be used only in this subtab's balance sheet ratios.

- There are two sets of results available. The first and larger results grid shows the time series of cash flow analysis for the Project for multiple years. These are the cash flows used to compute the NPV, IRR, MIRR, and so forth.

- The smaller grid at the bottom of the screen returns the balance sheet ratios, which apply the input parameters at the top of the tab. These are single-point estimates and represent a snapshot in time for either the firm or the project's balance sheet.

- The first project requires you to enter the eleven balance sheet input assumptions, whereas all other projects' balance sheet inputs either can be linked to the first project or uniquely entered (if these are projects under a different balance sheet scenario such as international projects or a different year). Use the *Link Input Assumptions from Project 1* or *Use Custom Input Assumptions* droplist to select the relevant settings you need.

- You can show the results as cash flow values and ratios or as percentage of sales revenue (use the *Show Earnings and Cash Flow Values* droplist to make your selection).

This *Economic Results* (Level 3) subtab shows the results from the chosen Project and returns the Net Present Value (NPV), Internal Rate of Return (IRR), Modified Internal Rate of Return (MIRR), Profitability Index (PI), Return on Investment (ROI), Payback Period (PP), and Discounted Payback Period (DPP), as seen in Figure 3.3. Refer to the previous chapter for details on each of the calculation methods.

An NPV Profile table and chart are also provided, where different discount rates and their respective NPV results are shown and charted. You can change the range of the discount rates to show/compute, copy the results, and copy the NPV Profile chart, as well as use any of the chart icons to manipulate the chart's look and feel (e.g., change the chart's line/background color, chart type, chart view, or add/remove gridlines, labels, and legend). You can also change the variable to display in the chart. For instance, you can change the chart from displaying the NPV Profile to the time-series charts of net cash flows, escalated net cash flows, taxable income, final cash flows, cumulative final cash flows, or present value of the final cash flows. You can then click on the *Copy Chart* button to take a screenshot of the modified chart that you can then paste into another software application such as Microsoft Excel or Microsoft PowerPoint. As a note of caution, when you click this *Copy Chart* button, please do give it an extra second before moving the mouse and pasting into another software because on slower computers, the native Windows imager services will need to run in the background and may take the added second or two to complete.

Figure 3.1 – DCF Model: Project Input Assumptions

[EXAMPLE] - PROJECT ECONOMICS ANALYSIS TOOL

File Edit Projects Report Tools Language Decimals Help

Welcome to the ROV Project Economics Analysis Tool (PEAT). This module will help you set up a series of projects or Capital Investment Options, model their Cash Flows, Simulate Risks, and run Advanced Analytics; perform Forecasting and Prediction Modeling; and Optimize your Investment Portfolio subject to budgetary and other Constraints.

Discounted Cash Flow   Applied Analytics   Risk Simulation   Options Valuation   Forecast Prediction   Portfolio Optimization   Dashboard   Knowledge Center.

Custom (d61)   Project 1   Project 2   Project 3   Project 4   Project 5   Project 6   Project 7   Project 8   Project 9   Project 10   Portfolio Analysis   Discount Rates

1. Discounted Cash Flow Model (DCF)   2. Cash Flow Ratios   3. Economic Results   4. Information and Details

DCF Starting Year 2016   DCF Ending Year 2043   Discount Rate (%) 10.00%   Marginal Tax Rate (%) 28.50%   Scenario / Forex   Notes:

Revenues: 1 Rows   Direct Costs: 6 Rows   Indirect Expenses: 4 Rows   Capex Rows: 1   View Full Grid   Allow Negative Taxes

Year	2016	2017	2018	2019	2020	2021	2022	2023	2024	2
Revenues	1,742.50	11,737.14	225,850.12	225,850.12	225,850.12	225,850.12	225,850.12	225,850.12	225,850.12	225
Sales Revenue - Global Sales	1,742.50	11,737.14	225,850.12	225,850.12	225,850.12	225,850.12	225,850.12	225,850.12	225,850.12	225
Direct Costs	1,141.09	1,141.09	26,392.75	26,392.75	26,392.75	26,456.81	27,888.82	27,888.82	27,888.82	27.
Direct R&D	1,110.26	1,110.26	24,896.68	24,896.68	24,896.68	24,896.68	24,896.68	24,896.68	24,896.68	24,
Manufacturing	18.50	18.50	414.95	414.95	414.95	453.38	829.89	829.89	829.89	8.
Fabrication	12.33	12.33	25.62	25.62	25.62	51.25	51.25	51.25	51.25	5
Direct COGS	0.00	0.00	1,055.50	1,055.50	1,055.50	1,055.50	2,111.00	2,111.00	2,111.00	2,
Gross Profit (Operating Income)	601.41	10,596.05	199,457.37	199,457.37	199,457.37	199,393.31	197,961.30	197,961.30	197,961.30	197
Indirect Expenses (General & Administrative)	799.42	3,073.28	9,212.61	9,212.61	9,212.61	9,212.61	9,212.61	10,877.49	9,567.71	9,5
Sales and Administrative	0.00	31.00	703.00	703.00	703.00	703.00	703.00	703.00	703.00	7.
Marketing and Advertising	0.00	0.00	0.00	0.00	0.00	0.00	0.00	0.00	0.00	
Operations	0.00	0.00	1,248.07	1,248.07	1,248.07	1,248.07	1,248.07	1,248.07	1,248.07	1,2
Maintenance	799.42	2,997.82	4,758.48	4,758.48	4,758.48	4,758.48	4,758.48	6,423.36	5,113.58	5;
Foreign Transactions	0.00	0.00	1,506.00	1,506.00	1,506.00	1,506.00	1,506.00	1,506.00	1,506.00	1,!
Channel Partners	0.00	44.46	997.06	997.06	997.06	997.06	997.06	997.06	997.06	9!
EBITDA: Earnings Before Interest, Taxes, Depreciation, and Amortization	-198.01	7,522.77	190,244.76	190,244.76	190,244.76	190,180.70	188,748.69	187,083.81	188,393.59	188
Depreciation	0.00	9,874.00	39,827.00	39,074.00	38,161.00	37,206.00	36,172.00	35,223.00	34,476.00	33,
Amortization	0.00	0.00	0.00	0.00	0.00	0.00	0.00	0.00	0.00	
EBIT: Earnings Before Interest and Taxes	-198.01	-2,351.23	150,417.76	151,170.76	152,083.76	152,974.70	152,576.69	151,860.81	153,915.59	154

Welcome to the ROV Project Economics Analysis Tool (PEAT). This module will help you set up a series of projects or Capital Investment Options, model their Cash Flows, Simulate Risks, and run Advanced Analytics; perform Forecasting and Prediction Modeling; and Optimize your Investment Portfolio subject to Budgetary and other Constraints.

Discounted Cash Flow   Applied Analytics   Risk Simulation   Options Strategies   Options Valuation   Forecast Prediction   Portfolio Optimization   Dashboard   Knowledge Centre.

Custom (xlsx)   Project 1   Project 2   Project 3   Project 4   Project 5   Project 6   Project 7   Project 8   Project 9   Project 10   Portfolio Analysis   Discount Rates

1. Discounted Cash Flow Model (DCF)   2. Cash Flow Ratios   3. Economic Results   4. Information and Details

Current Asset	32,806.00	Current Liabilities	18,370.00	Long-Term Operating Assets	114,095.00	Total Inventories	676.61
Accounts Receivables	4,016.00	Shares Outstanding	1,132,357,090.00	Stock Price Per Share	27.00	Common Equity	70,530.00
Total Assets	146,901.00	Total Debt	58,001.00	Total Net Operating Capital	128,531.00		

Show Earnings and Cash Flow Values   View Full Grid

Year	Average	Median	2016	2017	2018	2019	2020	2021	2022	2023	2024
EARNINGS BEFORE INT, TAX, DEP, AMORT (EBITDA)	177,349.56	190,837.40	-198.01	7,522.77	190,244.76	190,244.76	190,244.76	190,180.70	188,748.69	187,083.81	188,393.59	18...
EARNINGS BEFORE INTEREST AND TAXES (EBIT)	148,538.46	160,170.90	-198.01	-2,351.23	150,417.76	151,170.76	152,083.76	152,974.70	152,576.69	151,860.81	153,915.59	15...
NET INCOME (NI)	102,215.90	114,057.53	-141.58	-6,528.34	89,035.45	91,808.58	94,994.48	98,049.50	99,753.00	99,783.27	101,776.22	10...
NET OPERATING PROFIT AFTER TAXES (NOPAT)	106,205.00	114,522.19	-141.58	-1,681.13	107,548.70	108,087.09	108,739.89	109,376.91	109,092.33	108,580.48	110,049.65	11...
NET CASH FLOW (NCF)	131,027.00	144,724.03	-141.58	3,345.66	128,862.45	130,882.58	133,155.48	135,255.50	135,925.00	135,006.27	136,254.22	13...
OPERATING CASH FLOW (OCF)	135,016.10	145,188.69	-141.58	8,192.87	147,375.70	147,161.09	146,900.89	146,582.91	145,264.33	143,803.48	144,527.65	14...
FREE CASH FLOW (FCF)	135,016.10	145,188.69	-141.58	8,192.87	147,375.70	147,161.09	146,900.89	146,582.91	145,264.33	143,803.48	144,527.65	14...
RETURN ON INVESTED CAPITAL (ROIC)	82.63%	89.10%	-0.11%	-1.31%	83.68%	84.09%	84.60%	85.10%	84.88%	84.48%	85.62%	8
ECONOMIC VALUE ADDED (EVA)	93,351.90	101,669.09	-12,994.68	-14,534.23	94,695.60	95,233.99	95,886.79	96,523.81	96,239.23	95,727.38	97,196.55	97
TIMES INTEREST EARNED (TIE)	147.91	246.46	0	-0.35	5.81	6.64	7.91	9.66	11.68	12.34	13.30	
NET PROFIT MARGIN (NPM)	42.01%	49.04%	-8.12%	-55.62%	39.42%	40.65%	42.06%	43.41%	44.17%	44.18%	45.06%	4
OPERATING PROFIT MARGIN (OPM)	45.17%	49.24%	-8.12%	-14.32%	47.62%	47.86%	48.15%	48.43%	48.30%	48.08%	48.73%	4

Balance Sheet Ratios

CURRENT RATIO (CR)	1.79	BOOK VALUE PER SHARE (BV)	0.00
QUICK RATIO (QR)	1.75	DEBT TO ASSET RATIO	39.48%
NET OPERATING WORKING CAPITAL (NOWC)	14,436.00	MARKET TO BOOK RATIO (MB)	433,484.21
NET OPERATING CAPITAL (NOC)	128,531.00	EQUITY MULTIPLIER (EM)	2.08
MARKET VALUE ADDED (MVA)	30,573,570,900.00	DEBT TO EQUITY RATIO (DE)	0.82

Figure 3.2 – DCF Model: Cash Flow Ratios

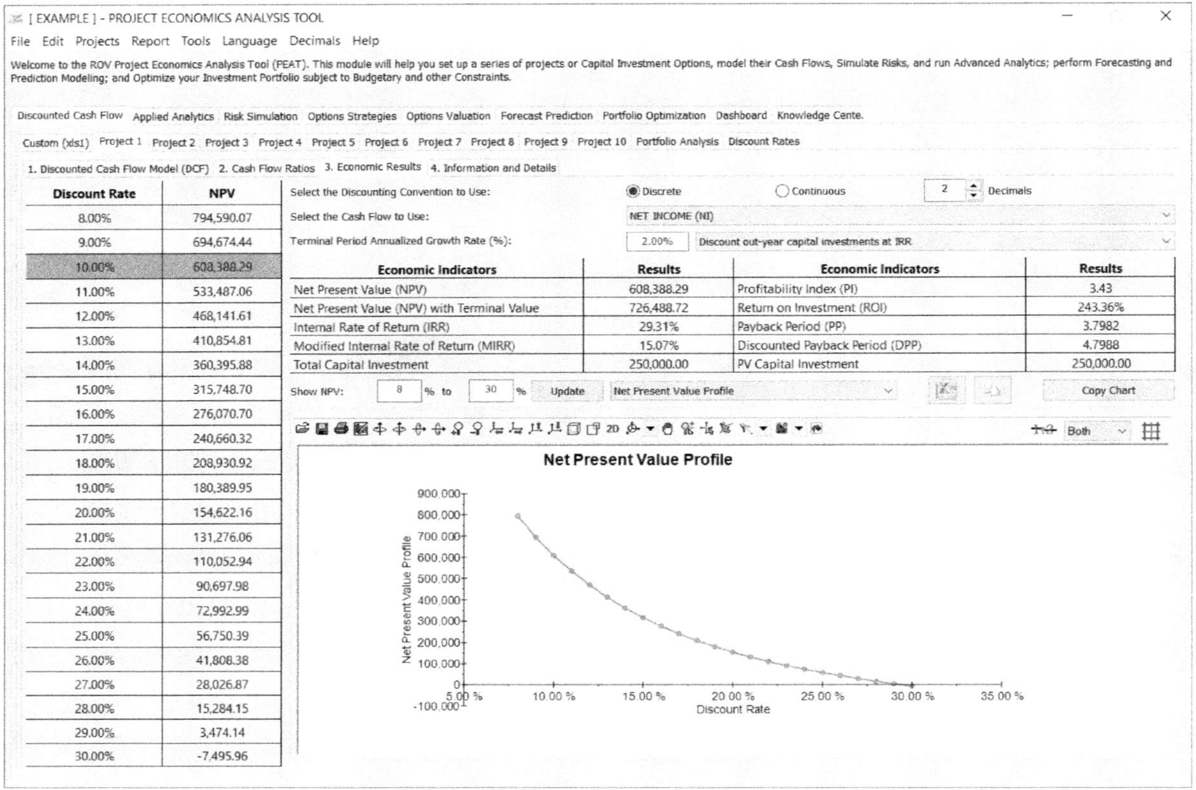
[EXAMPLE] - PROJECT ECONOMICS ANALYSIS TOOL
File Edit Projects Report Tools Language Decimals Help
Welcome to the ROV Project Economics Analysis Tool (PEAT). This module will help you set up a series of projects or Capital Investment Options, model their Cash Flows, Simulate Risks, and run Advanced Analytics; perform Forecasting and Prediction Modeling; and Optimize your Investment Portfolio subject to Budgetary and other Constraints.
Discounted Cash Flow Applied Analytics Risk Simulation Options Strategies Options Valuation Forecast Prediction Portfolio Optimization Dashboard Knowledge Cente.
Custom (xls1) Project 1 Project 2 Project 3 Project 4 Project 5 Project 6 Project 7 Project 8 Project 9 Project 10 Portfolio Analysis Discount Rates
1. Discounted Cash Flow Model (DCF) 2. Cash Flow Ratios 3. Economic Results 4. Information and Details
Discount Rate NPV
8.00% 794,590.07
9.00% 694,674.44
10.00% 608,388.29
11.00% 533,487.06
12.00% 468,141.61
13.00% 410,854.81
14.00% 360,395.88
15.00% 315,748.70
16.00% 276,070.70
17.00% 240,660.32
18.00% 208,930.92
19.00% 180,389.95
20.00% 154,622.16
21.00% 131,276.06
22.00% 110,052.94
23.00% 90,697.98
24.00% 72,992.99
25.00% 56,750.39
26.00% 41,808.38
27.00% 28,026.87
28.00% 15,284.15
29.00% 3,474.14
30.00% -7,495.96
Select the Discounting Convention to Use: Discrete Continuous 2 Decimals
Select the Cash Flow to Use: NET INCOME (NI)
Terminal Period Annualized Growth Rate (%): 2.00% Discount out-year capital investments at IRR
Economic Indicators Results Economic Indicators Results
Net Present Value (NPV) 608,388.29 Profitability Index (PI) 3.43
Net Present Value (NPV) with Terminal Value 726,488.72 Return on Investment (ROI) 243.36%
Internal Rate of Return (IRR) 29.31% Payback Period (PP) 3.7982
Modified Internal Rate of Return (MIRR) 15.07% Discounted Payback Period (DPP) 4.7988
Total Capital Investment 250,000.00 PV Capital Investment 250,000.00
Show NPV: 8 % to 30 % Update Net Present Value Profile Copy Chart
Both
Net Present Value Profile
Net Present Value Profile
900,000
800,000
700,000
600,000
500,000
400,000
300,000
200,000
100,000
0
-100,000
5.00 % 10.00 % 15.00 % 20.00 % 25.00 % 30.00 % 35.00 %
Discount Rate

Figure 3.3 – DCF Model: Economic Results

Here are some additional tips working in this *Economic Results* tab:

- The *Economic Results* are for each individual Project, whereas the *Portfolio Analysis* tab compares the economic results of all Projects at once.

- The Terminal Value Annualized Growth Rate is applied to the last year's cash flow to account for a perpetual constant growth rate cash flow model, and these future cash flows are discounted back to the base year and added to the NPV to arrive at the NPV with Terminal Value result. The Gordon Growth Model is used to calculate the terminal value and then its result is discounted back to the starting year.

- You can change the *Show NPV* percentages and click *Update* to change the NPV Profile results grid and chart (assuming you selected the NPV Profile chart, as shown in Figure 3. 3).

- As usual, there are *chart icons* for you to modify the chart (bar chart color, chart type, chart view, background color, rotation, show/hide labels and legends, show/hide gridlines and data labels, etc.). Also available are the *Copy Results* and *Copy Chart* functionalities. Again, on slower or older computers, remember to give it an additional second after you click on *Copy Chart* before moving the mouse and pasting into another application.

- There is a *discount out-year capital investments* drop-down list using the IRR Method or Discount Rate Method. The IRR result that is computed will depend on the method chosen. The traditional method is to use IRR as the reinvestment rate (default selection in the drop-down list) defined as the discount rate where the NPV = 0 (this can be verified in the NPV and Discount Rate grid on the left of the screen). This approach works in most traditional models but will return a null result if the IRR requirement is violated. IRR has a requirement that the initial Cash Flow (CF) at time 0 compared to Capital Investments (INV) at time 0 be such that $INV_0 > CF_0$, otherwise the concept of IRR and its math do not work. This method works well in most business situations (capital investments come early, and positive cash flows come later in time), but one can also have a situation where $INV_0 < CF_0$, making the *Total Net Cash Flow* or CF_0

$- INV_0 > 0$. Therefore, the traditional IRR, defined as the Discount Rate where NPV $= 0$, will not return a valid result (this situation of the initial cash flow being greater than the investment can, in fact, occur in real-life, albeit seldom). There are two ways to solve this problem. The first is that you manually push the positive CF_0 one period into the future using some discount rate or reinvestment rate or discount all future INV_T amounts at the discount rate back to time zero, thereby making the *Total Net Cash Flow* or CF_0 $- INV_0 < 0$ as the present value of the $\Sigma INV_T > CF_0$. This is essentially the approach undertaken in the second item on the drop-down list (please be aware that in this situation, the computed IRR is really a quasi-IRR and therefore will not be the discount rate making the NPV $= 0$; it will, nonetheless, at least provide you a computed metric). Of course, in a highly profitable project where the present value of the $\Sigma INV_T < CF_0$, neither the traditional IRR nor the quasi-IRR works.

- o IRR calculations require that *Total Initial Cash Flow* $(CF_0 - INV_0) < 0$. This value has to be NEGATIVE.

- o The IRR Method stops if $(CF_0 > INV_0)$ or NET $CF_0 > 0$. This value cannot be POSITIVE.

- o The IRR Method is better in most cases except when the following occurs, then the IRR Method cannot return a value, and only the Discount Rate Method will return a result (although this is a quasi-IRR and not the traditional IRR): $(CF_0 > INV_0)$ or NET $CF_0 > 0$, and if *Present Value of the* $\Sigma INV_T > CF_0$.

- o If *Present Value of the* $\Sigma INV_T < CF_0$, neither method works.

To summarize, we see the following effects on IRR calculations:

No Cash Flow at Time 0 ($CF_0 = 0$):

Large Investments in Year 0
    IRR Method = DR Method, both work, same results
Large Investments in Year 0, 2, 5
    IRR Method runs and is correct;
    DR Method runs quasi-IRR
Large Investments in Year 2, 5
    IRR Method runs and is correct;
    DR Method runs quasi-IRR
Small Investments in Year 0
    IRR Method = DR Method, both work, same results
Small Investments in Year 0, 2, 5
    IRR Method runs and is correct;
    DR Method runs quasi-IRR
Small Investments in Year 2, 5
    IRR Method cannot compute;
    DR Method cannot compute

Some Cash Flow at Time 0 ($CF_0 > 0$):

Large Investments in Year 0
    IRR Method = DR Method, both work, same results
Large Investments in Year 0, 2, 5
    IRR Method runs and is correct;
    DR Method runs quasi-IRR
Large Investments in Year 2, 5
    IRR Method cannot compute;
    DR Method runs quasi-IRR
Small Investments in Year 0
    IRR Method cannot compute;
    DR Method cannot compute
Small Investments in Year 0, 2, 5
    IRR Method cannot compute;
    DR Method runs quasi-IRR
Small Investments in Year 2, 5
    IRR Method cannot compute;
    DR Method cannot compute

Project | Information and Details

In this tab, you can enter information and notes of the Project. The default settings have category labels such as Project Title, Corporate Objective, and so forth. You can click on the *Categories* button to modify these category titles (Figure 3.4).

- Use this tab for entering justifications for the input assumptions used as well as any notes on each of the Projects. For numerical calculations and notes, use the *Custom Calculations* tab instead.

- You can also change the labels and categories of the Information and Details tab by clicking on *Categories* and editing the labels.

- The formatting of entered text can be performed in the Description box by clicking on the various *text formatting icons*.

Project | Portfolio Analysis

The *Portfolio Analysis* tab (Figure 3.5) returns the computed economic and financial indicators such as NPV, IRR, MIRR, PI, ROI, PP, and DPP for all the Projects combined into a portfolio view. The Economic Results (Level 3) subtabs show the individual Project's economic and financial indicators, whereas this Level 2 Portfolio Analysis view shows the results of all Projects' indicators and compares them side by side. There are also two charts available for comparing these individual Projects' results.

- The *Portfolio Analysis* tab is used to obtain a side-by-side comparison of all the main economic and financial indicators of all the Projects at once. For instance, you can compare all the NPVs from each Project in a single results grid.

- What appears to be a chart graphic in the upper right (Figure 3.5 shows the DCF module's default example's Portfolio Analysis results) is actually a placeholder such that when there are multiple Projects, the data results grid will expand in width to cover said graphic.

- The bubble chart on the left provides a visual representation of three main variables at once (e.g., the y-axis shows the IRR, the x-axis represents the NPV, and the size of the bubble may represent the capital investment; in such a situation, one would prefer a smaller ball that is in the top right quadrant of the chart). As usual, *chart icons, Copy Grid,* and *Copy Chart* are available for use in this tab.

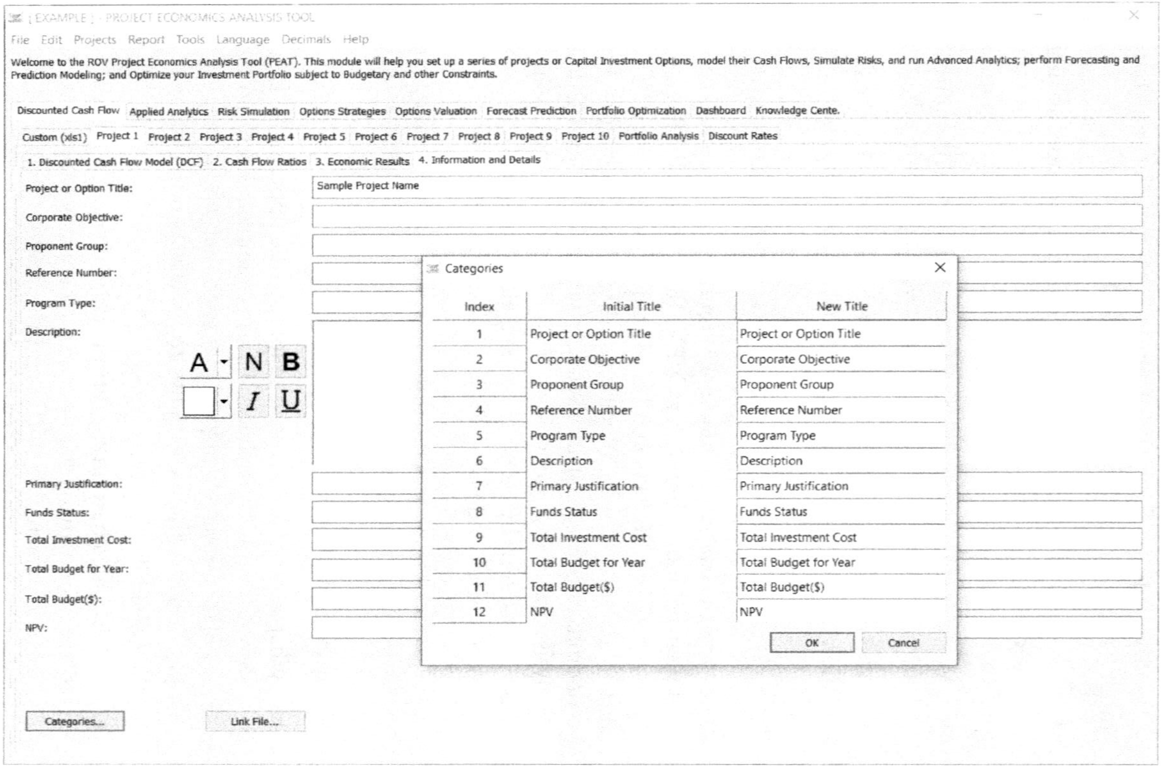

Figure 3.4 – Information and Details

[EXAMPLE 1] - PROJECT ECONOMICS ANALYSIS TOOL

File   Edit   Projects   Report   Tools   Language   Decimals   Help

Welcome to the ROV Project Economics Analysis Tool (PEAT). This module will help you set up a series of projects or Capital Investment Options, model their Cash Flows, Simulate Risks, and run Advanced Analytics; perform Forecasting and Prediction Modeling; and Optimize your Investment Portfolio subject to Budgetary and other Constraints.

Discounted Cash Flow   Applied Analytics   Risk Simulation   Options Valuation   Options Strategies   Forecast Prediction   Portfolio Analysis   Portfolio Optimization   Dashboard   Knowledge Centre.

Custom (xlsx)   Project 1   Project 2   Project 3   Project 4   Project 5   Project 6   Project 7   Project 8   Project 9   Project 10   Portfolio Analysis   Discount Rates

Analysis of Alternatives (No Base Case)
Incremental Analysis (Choose Base Case):

Economic Results		Project 1	Project 2	Project 3	Project 4	Project 5	Project 6	Project 7	Project 8	Project 9	Project 10
Net Present Value (NPV)		608,388.29	205,972.62	31,361.10	30,667.51	93,176.36	69,507.57	728,339.38	361,833.73	19,853.65	36,046.39
Net Present Value (NPV) with Terminal Value		726,488.72	310,848.95	59,306.45	52,893.78	154,272.47	-22,422.35	1,124,579.59	538,114.39	145,111.43	351,581.73
Internal Rate of Return (IRR)		29.31%	10.58%	14.75%	16.80%	28.16%	29.92%	11.20%	12.43%	7.69%	12.81%
Modified Internal Rate of Return (MIRR)		15.07%	10.21%	11.91%	12.50%	15.21%	17.36%	10.39%	10.88%	6.23%	9.17%
Profitability Index (PI)		3.43	1.07	1.29	1.39	1.84	1.94	1.09	1.19	1.21	1.59
Return on Investment (ROI)		243.36%	6.68%	28.72%	39.46%	83.92%	93.70%	9.00%	19.12%	21.33%	59.04%
Payback Period (PP)		3.7982	11.2820	6.8823	6.1294	3.7760	3.5519	9.9783	8.6055	10.2103	8.1262
Discounted Payback Period (DPP)		4.7988	26.5103	11.1445	9.3080	4.8017	4.4399	22.3462	16.5935	14.1122	10.5357

Project 1

Update

Show Grid

Show on Charts

Net Present Value (NPV) with Terminal Value
Investment Portfolio View

Net Present Value (IRR)

Charts...   Copy Chart

Net Present Value (NPV)
Net Present Value (NPV)

Charts...   2D Bar

Copy Chart

Investment Portfolio View

- Project 1
- Project 2
- Project 3
- Project 4
- Project 5
- Project 6
- Project 7
- Project 8
- Project 9
- Project 10

Internal Rate of Return (IRR)

Net Present Value (NPV) with Terminal Value

Net Present Value (NPV)

Projects

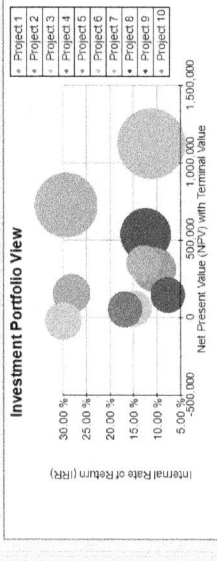

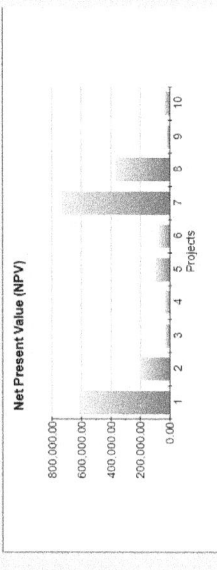

Figure 3.5 – Portfolio Analysis

4

APPLIED ANALYTICS

The *Applied Analytics* section allows you to run Tornado Analysis and Scenario Analysis on any one of the Projects previously modeled— this analytics tab is on Level 1, which means it covers all of the various Projects on Level 2. You can, therefore, run Tornado or Scenario on any one of the Projects.

Applied Analytics | Static Tornado

Tornado Analysis (Figure 4.1 shows the DCF module's default example's Tornado Analysis result) is a static sensitivity analysis of the selected model's output to each input assumption, performed one at a time, and ranked from most impactful to the least. Start the analysis by first choosing the output variable to test from the drop-down list.

You can change the default sensitivity settings of each input assumption to test and decide how many input assumption variables to chart (large models with many inputs may generate unsightly and less useful charts, whereas showing just the top variables reveals more information through a more elegant chart). You can also choose to run the input assumptions as unique inputs, group them as a line item (all individual inputs on a single line item are assumed to be one variable), or run as variable groups (e.g., all line items under Revenue will be assumed to be a single variable). Remember to click *Compute* to update the analysis if you make any changes to any of the settings. The sensitivity results are also shown as a table grid at the bottom of the screen (e.g., the initial base value of the chosen output variable, the input assumption changes, and the resulting output variable's sensitivity results). As usual, you can *Copy Chart* or *Copy Grid* results into the Windows clipboard for pasting into another software application.

- Each horizontal bar indicates a unique input assumption that constitutes a precedent to the selected output variable.

- The x-axis represents the values of the selected output variable. The wider the bar chart, the greater the impact/swing the input assumption has on the output.

- A green bar on the right indicates that the input assumption has a positive effect on the selected output (conversely, a red bar indicates a negative effect).

- As another example, in Figure 4.1, we see the following:

  o The output tested is Project 1's NPV with Terminal Value.

  o Each of the precedent or input assumptions that directly affects the NPV with Terminal Value is tested ±10%; the top 10 variables are shown on the chart, with a 2 decimal precision setting, and each unique input is tested individually.

  o The results indicate that the Discount Rate has the highest impact, naturally, with the highest swing (widest horizontal bar), with a red bar on the right, indicating that the lower the discount rate (*Input Downside* in the grid and on the red right chart: 9.00%), the higher the NPV (*Output Downside* in the grid and on the red right bar chart's x-axis: 867,389). Conversely, the higher the discount rate (*Input Upside* in the grid and on the green left bar chart: 11.00%), the lower the NPV (*Output Upside* in the grid and on the red right bar chart's x-axis: 615,707).

- The Excel icon will create a live Excel-based Tornado chart.

- Multiple chart icons are available to manipulate the look and feel of the chart (e.g., the ABC… icon will change the vertical axis labels between the shortened and detailed description).

- You can also create and save multiple Tornado charts using the saved models section at the bottom right of the software.

Scenario Analysis can be easily performed through a two-step process: set up the model and run the model. In the *Scenario Input Settings* subtab (Figure 4.2 shows the DCF module's default example's Scenario Input Settings), start by selecting the output variable you wish to test from the drop-down list. Then, based on your selection, the precedents of the output will be listed under two categories (*Line Item*, which will change all input assumptions in the entire line item in the model simultaneously, and *Single Item*, which will change individual input assumption items). *Select one or two checkboxes* at a time and the inputs you wish to run scenarios on and enter the plus/minus percentage to test and the number of steps between these two values to test. You can also *add color coding* of sweetspots or hotspots in the scenario analysis (values falling within different ranges have unique colors). You can create multiple scenarios and *Save As* each one (enter a *Name* for each saved scenario).

Proceed to the *Scenario Output Tables* (Figure 4.3) to run the saved analysis. Click on the *drop-down list* to select the previously saved scenarios to run. The selected scenario table complete with sweetspot/hotspot color coding will be generated. *Decimals* can be increased or decreased as required, and you can *Copy Grid* or *View Full Grid* as needed. To facilitate review of the scenario tables, pay attention to the NOTE, which provides the information of which input variable is set as the rows versus columns.

Here are some additional tips:

- You can create and run *Scenario Analysis* on either one or two input variables at once.

- The scenario settings can be saved for retrieval in the future, which means you can modify any input assumptions in the Projects' models and come back to rerun the saved scenarios.

- You can also *increase/decrease decimals* in the scenario results tables, as well as change colors in the tables for easier visual interpretation (especially when trying to identify scenario combinations, or so-called sweetspots and hotspots).

- Remember to scroll down the form for additional input variables.

- *Line Items* can be changed using $\pm X\%$ where all inputs in the line are changed multiple times within this specific range all at once. *Individual Items* can be changed $\pm Y$ *units* where each input is changed multiple times within this specific range.

- You can either double-click on a saved model to retrieve its settings or click on the *Edit* button to edit the settings. Do not forget to click *Save* to save any changes you made or use *Save As* to duplicate the model and create a new model with the modified settings.

- Sweetspots and hotspots refer to specific combinations of two input variables that will drive the output up or down. For instance, suppose investments are below a certain threshold and revenues are above a certain barrier, then the NPV will be in excess of the expected budget (the sweetspots, perhaps highlighted in green), or if investments are above a certain value, NPV will turn negative if revenues fall below a certain threshold (the hotspots, perhaps high-lighted in red).

Welcome to the ROV Project Economics Analysis Tool (PEAT). This module will help you set up a series of projects or Capital Investment Options, model their Cash Flows, Simulate Risks, and run Advanced Analytics; perform Forecasting and Prediction Modeling; and Optimize your Investment Portfolio subject to Budgetary and other Constraints.

Discounted Cash Flow   Applied Analytics   Risk Simulation   Options Valuation   Options Strategies   Forecast Prediction   Portfolio Optimization   Dashboard   Knowledge Center

Static Tornado   Scenario Analysis

Tornado or static sensitivity analysis is performed by perturbing the inputs a preset amount one at a time to determine the impact on the output variable. Start by selecting the Option and Output Variable to test, then set the sensitivity levels and click Compute to run.

Select the Option and Output Variable to run:

Project 1: Net Present Value (NPV) with Terminal Value

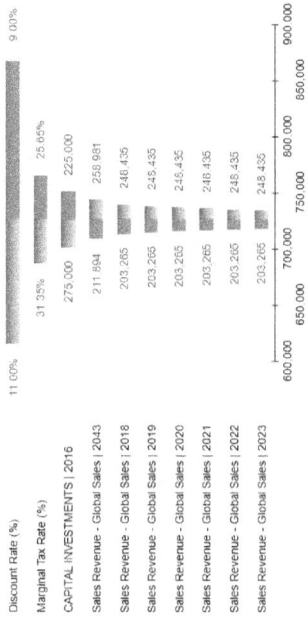

Sensitivity +/-   10   %
Show the top   10   variables
Show results with   2   decimals

Select the granularity of the sensitivity analysis:

● Individual Unique Inputs
○ Line Items
○ Variable Groups

Update   Excel   Copy Chart

The Tornado run has been completed. Tornado Running Time: 2s.

Show results with   2   decimals

Project 1: Net Present Value (NPV) with Terminal Value

Discount Rate (%)   11.00%
Marginal Tax Rate (%)   31.35%

CAPITAL INVESTMENTS | 2016		275.000	225.000	
Sales Revenue - Global Sales | 2043		211.894	258.981	
Sales Revenue - Global Sales | 2018		203.265	248.435	
Sales Revenue - Global Sales | 2019		203.265	248.435	
Sales Revenue - Global Sales | 2020		203.265	248.435	
Sales Revenue - Global Sales | 2021		203.265	248.435	
Sales Revenue - Global Sales | 2022		203.265	248.435	
Sales Revenue - Global Sales | 2023		203.265	248.435	

600.000   650.000   700.000   750.000   800.000   850.000   900.000

Name: NPV Project 4

New   Save As
Edit
Save
Delete

Model
NPV Project 1
NPV Project 2 - Line Items
IRR Project 3 - Unique Inputs
NPV Project 4

Base Value: 726,488.72

				Changes		
Chart	% Up	% Down	Inputs	Output Down	Output Up	Range	Input Down	Input Up	Base Case
✓	10.00%	10.00%	Discount Rate (%)	867,389.62	615,707.74	251,681.88	9.00%	11.00%	10.00%
✓	10.00%	10.00%	Marginal Tax Rate (%)	765,411.70	687,565.75	77,845.95	23.65%	31.35%	28.50%
✓	10.00%	10.00%	CAPITAL INVESTMENTS | 2016	751,488.72	701,488.72	50,000.00	225,000.00	275,000.00	250,000.00
✓	10.00%	10.00%	Sales Revenue - Global Sales | 2043	708,833.15	744,144.29	35,311.14	211,893.70	258,981.18	235,437.44
✓	10.00%	10.00%	Sales Revenue - Global Sales | 2018	713,143.04	739,834.41	26,691.38	203,265.11	248,435.13	225,850.12

Figure 4.1 – Static Tornado Analysis

[EXAMPLE] - PROJECT ECONOMICS ANALYSIS TOOL

File   Edit   Projects   Report   Tools   Language   Decimals   Help

Welcome to the ROV Project Economics Analysis Tool (PEAT). This module will help you set up a series of projects or Capital Investment Options, model their Cash Flows, Simulate Risks, and run Advanced Analytics; perform Forecasting and Prediction Modeling; and Optimize your Investment Portfolio subject to Budgetary and other Constraints.

Discounted Cash Flow   Applied Analytics   Risk Simulation   Options Strategies   Options Valuation   Forecast Prediction   Portfolio Optimization   Dashboard   Knowledge Center

Static Tornado   Scenario Analysis

1. Scenario Input Settings   2. Scenario Output Tables ("Sweetspots")

Scenario Analysis helps identify the sweetspots and hotspots in the results based on different inputs. Select the Option and Output Variable you wish to analyze and from the list of input variables, select up to TWO variables to change (check the box and enter the From, To, Step Size). You can add color coding to identify potential sweetspots and hotspots, and save the scenario settings for future runs.

OPTIONAL: Color-coding "sweetspots" and "hotspots".

	if value is	less than		0.06	&
Color cell ■	if value is	between		8.00	&
Color cell □	if value is	between		50,000.00	&
Color cell ■	if value is	greater than		100,000.00	&
Color cell ■	if value is				&
Color cell ■					

Select Option and Output Variable:

Project 1: Net Present Value (NPV)   608,388.29

SAVE:

Name:
Notes:

Save As...

Edit
Save
Delete

Revenue vs Discount Rate

Name
Revenue vs Discount Rate
USA Revenue vs Global Discount Rate

Line Item	Original Value	- %	+ %	Step Size
Revenues | Sales Revenue - Global Sales	6,021,645.11	-5.00%	+5.00%	0.50%
Direct Costs | Direct R&D	664,649.46	-5%	+5%	0.50%
Direct Costs | Manufacturing	32,225.76	-5%	+5%	0.50%
Direct Costs | Fabrication	2,082.90	-5%	+5%	0.50%
Direct Costs | Direct COGS	79,162.55	-5%	+5%	0.50%
Indirect Expenses | Sales and Administrative	18,737.00	-5%	+5%	0.50%
Indirect Expenses | Marketing and Advertising	0.00	-5%	+5%	0.50%
Indirect Expenses | Operations	32,449.82	-5%	+5%	0.50%
Indirect Expenses | Maintenance	160,820.52	-5%	+5%	0.50%
Indirect Expenses | Foreign Transactions	39,156.00	-5%	+5%	0.50%
Indirect Expenses | Channel Partners	26,573.31	-5%	+5%	0.50%
DCF | Depreciation	806,711.00	-5%	+5%	0.50%
DCF | Amortization	0.00	-5%	+5%	0.50%
DCF | Interest	156,216.53	-5%	+5%	0.50%
DCF | Change in Net Working Capital	0.00	-5%	+5%	0.50%
DCF | Capital Expenditures	0.00	-5%	+5%	0.50%

Figure 4.2 – Scenario Analysis: Scenario Input Settings

Welcome to the ROV Project Economics Analysis Tool (PEAT). This module will help you set up a series of projects or Capital Investment Options, model their Cash Flows, Simulate Risks, and run Advanced Analytics; perform Forecasting and Prediction Modeling; and Optimize your Investment Portfolio subject to Budgetary and other Constraints.

Discounted Cash Flow   Applied Analytics   Risk Simulation   Options Strategies   Options Valuation   Forecast Prediction   Portfolio Optimization   Dashboard   Knowledge Center

Static Tornado   Scenario Analysis

1. Scenario Input Settings   2. Scenario Output Tables ("Sweetspots")

Select one of the saved scenarios to run the scenario table. In the event you make any changes in the inputs or settings, remember to click Update to manually update the scenario table.

Select the Seved Scenario to Compute:

Show results with [0] decimals

NOTE: The Row variable (down) is

Scenario table is for: Revenue vs Discount Rate

Revenues | Sales Revenue - Global Sales   and the Column variable (across) is   DCF | Discount Rate (%)

Project 1: Net Present Value (NPV)

	20.00%	21.00%	22.00%	23.00%	24.00%	25.00%	26.00%	27.00%	28.00%	29.00%	30.00%
5,720,563	120,704	99,179	79,617	61,782	45,473	30,515	16,759	4,074.7			
5,750,671	124,096	102,388	82,660	64,674	48,225	33,139	19,264	6,469.9			
5,780,779	127,488	105,598	85,704	67,565	50,977	35,762	21,769	8,865.1	1,063.1		
5,810,888	130,880	108,806	88,748	70,457	53,729	38,386	24,274	11,260	2,684	1,197	
5,840,996	134,271	112,018	91,791	73,348	56,481	41,009	26,779	13,656	1,523.6	4,784	20,166
5,871,104	137,663	115,227	94,835	76,240	59,233	43,633	29,284	16,051	3,817.0	5,169.3	8,046
5,901,212	141,055	118,437	97,878	79,132	61,985	46,256	31,789	18,446	6,110.4	6,321.0	5,306
5,931,320	144,447	121,647	100,922	82,023	64,737	48,880	34,294	20,841	8,403.9	3,122.2	3,806
5,961,429	147,839	124,857	103,966	84,915	67,489	51,503	36,798	23,236	10,697	2,991	9,606.6
5,991,537	151,230	128,066	107,009	87,806	70,241	54,127	39,303	25,632	12,991	1,275.3	2,984
6,021,645	154,622	131,276	110,053	90,698	72,993	56,750	41,808	28,027	15,284	3,474.1	4,895.1
6,051,753	158,014	134,486	113,097	93,590	75,745	59,374	44,313	30,422	17,578	5,672.9	9,879
6,081,862	161,406	137,696	116,140	96,481	78,497	61,997	46,818	32,817	19,871	7,871.7	14,651
6,111,970	164,798	140,905	119,184	99,373	81,249	64,621	49,323	35,213	22,164	10,071	64
6,142,078	168,189	144,115	122,227	102,264	84,001	67,245	51,828	37,608	24,458	12,269	946.50
6,172,186	171,581	147,325	125,271	105,156	86,753	69,868	54,333	40,003	26,751	14,468	3,057.1
6,202,294	174,973	150,534	128,315	108,047	89,505	72,492	56,838	42,398	29,045	16,667	5,167.7

Update   View Full Grid

Figure 2.3 – Scenario Analysis: Scenario Output Tables

5

RISK SIMULATION

In the *Risk Simulation* section, you can set up and run Monte Carlo risk simulations on any of your Projects' inputs. Specifically, you can set up probability distribution assumptions on any combinations of inputs, run a risk simulation comprising thousands of trials, and retrieve the simulated forecast outputs as charts, statistics, probabilities, and confidence intervals in order to develop comprehensive risk profiles of the Projects.

Risk Simulation | Set Input Assumptions

In the *Set Input Assumptions* subtab, you start the simulation analysis by first setting simulation distributional inputs here (Figure 5.1 shows the DCF module's default example's Set Input Assumptions settings). Click on and *choose one Project at a time* to list the available input assumptions. Click on the *probability distribution icon* under the Settings header (see Figure 5.1 for the highlighted cell) for the relevant input assumption row, *select the probability distribution to use, and enter the relevant input parameters*. Continue setting as many simulation inputs as required (you can check/uncheck the inputs to simulate). Enter the *simulation trials* to run (start with 1,000 as initial test runs and use 10,000 for the final run as a rule of thumb for most models). You can also *Save As* the model (remember to provide it a *Name*). Then click on *Run Simulation*. Finally, in this tab, you can set simulation assumptions across multiple Projects and *Simulate All Options at Once*, apply a *Seed Value* to replicate the exact simulation results each time it is run, apply pairwise *Correlations* between simulation inputs, and *Edit* a previously saved simulation model. The following are some additional helpful tips:

- Refer to Dr. Johnathan Mun's *Modeling Risk, Third Edition* (Thomson-Shore, 2016) for more technical details on selecting and understanding probability distributions.

- Although the software supports up to 50 probability distributions, in general, the most commonly used and applied distributions include *Triangular, Normal,* and *Uniform.*

- If you have historical data available, use the Forecast Prediction tab to perform a *Distributional Fitting* to determine the best-fitting distribution to use as well as to estimate the selected distribution's input parameters.

- You can also *Extract Simulation Data* when the risk simulation run is complete, and the extracted data can be used for additional analysis as required.

- You can *Save* multiple simulation settings such that they can be retrieved, edited, and modified as required in the future.

- Remember to select either *Simulate All Options at Once* or *Simulate Selected Option Only*, depending on whether you wish to run a risk simulation on all the Projects that have predefined simulation assumptions or to run a simulation only on the current Project that is selected. Select and run all Projects at once if you will be using the results for setting up and running portfolio optimization later.

- The simulated results (e.g., distributional statistics, percentiles, confidence intervals, and probabilities) provide and create a risk profile of your Projects.

- Double-clicking on a saved simulation model will run the simulation (or simply select the saved model and click *Run Simulation*) or selecting a saved model and clicking the *Edit* button allows you to make changes to the saved model.

- You can also click on the *Defaults…* button to set assumptions on all inputs at once with some generic parameter inputs (e.g., set all as Triangular distributions with +/- 10% or the most likely values).

- The *Set Simulation Assumptions for Multiple Years* button allows you to quickly enter or paste multiple assumptions at once for variables with multiple years.

After the simulation completes its run, go to the *Simulation Results* tab (Figure 5.2 shows the DCF module's default example's risk simulation results after running the Simulate All Options at Once selection). First *select the output variable* you wish to display using the drop-down list. The percentiles and simulation statistics are presented on the right, and the simulation forecast chart is shown on the left. You can change the chart type (e.g., PDF, CDF), enter *Percentiles* (in %) or *Certainty Values* (in output units) on the bottom left of the screen (remember to click *Update* when done) to show their vertical lines on the chart, or compute/show the *Percentiles/Confidence* levels on the bottom right of the screen (select the type, *Two Tail, Left Tail, Right Tail,* then either enter the percentile values to auto compute the confidence interval, or enter the confidence desired to obtain the relevant percentiles). Note that the bottom right section for percentiles and confidence levels is used to both show the vertical lines on the chart as well as to compute the statistical results (i.e., entering the percentile value automatically computes the corresponding confidence value, whereas entering the confidence level automatically imputes the corresponding percentile value) as compared to the section on the bottom left where it is used only to draw the vertical lines on the chart.

You can also *Save* the simulated results and *Open* them at a later session, *Copy Chart* or *Copy Results* to the clipboard for pasting into another software application, *Extract Simulation Data* to paste into Excel for additional analysis, modify the chart using the chart icons, and so forth.

The simulation forecast chart is highly flexible in the sense that you can modify its look and feel (e.g., color, chart type, background, gridlines, rotation, chart view, data labels, etc.) using the chart icons. To illustrate, if you entered either a *Percentile* or *Certainty Value* at the bottom left of the screen and clicked *Update*, you can then click on *Custom Text Properties* (Figures 5.3 and 5.4), select the *Vertical Line*, type in some custom text, click on the *Properties* button to change the font size/color/type, or use the *A* icons to move the custom text's location. Please note that the custom text properties box will be empty unless you have at least one vertical line (bottom left section).

Finally, note that the *Simulation Results* forecast chart shows one output variable at a time, whereas the *Overlay Results* compares multiple simulated output forecasts at once.

EXAMPLES: PROJECT ECONOMICS ANALYSIS TOOL

Welcome to the ROV Project Economics Analysis Tool (PEAT). This module will help you set up a series of projects or Capital Investment Options, model their Cash Flows, Simulate Risks, and run Advanced Analytics; perform Forecasting and Prediction Modeling; and Optimize your Investment Portfolio subject to Budgetary and other Constraints.

Discounted Cash Flow   Applied Analytics   Risk Simulation   Simulation Results   Overlay Results   Analysis of Alternatives   Dynamic Sensitivity   Options Valuation   Forecast Prediction   Portfolio Optimization   Dashboard   Knowledge Center

Set Input Assumptions   Simulation Results   Overlay Results   Analysis of Alternatives   Dynamic Sensitivity

Select the Option to simulate and set the relevant distributional input assumptions. Then, run the simulation and review the results.

Step 1: Choose an Option to set input assumptions.   Step 2: Click on the distributional icon to set your simulation assumption. You can turn an assumption on or off using the checkbox.

Name
Project 1
Project 2
Project 3
Project 4
Project 5
Project 6
Project 7
Project 8
Project 9

Variable		Single Point	Settings	Simulation Parameter Information
DCF	Discount Rate (%)	✓	10.00%		Triangular	Minimum: 0.0500; Most Likely: 0.1000; ...
DCF	Marginal Tax Rate (%)	✓	28.50%		Triangular	Minimum: 0.1425; Most Likely: 0.2850...
Revenues	Sales Revenue - Global Sales	2016	✓	1,742.50		Triangular	Minimum: 871.2500; Most Likely: 1742...
Revenues	Sales Revenue - Global Sales	2017	✓	11,737.14		Triangular	Minimum: 5868.5700; Most Likely: 1173...
Revenues	Sales Revenue - Global Sales	2018	✓	225,850.12		Triangular	Minimum: 112925.0600; Most Likely: 22...
Revenues	Sales Revenue	✓			
Revenues	Sales Revenue	✓			
Revenues	Sales Revenue	✓			
Revenues	Sales Revenue	✓			
Revenues	Sales Revenue	✓			
Revenues	Sales Revenue	✓			
Revenues	Sales Revenue	✓			
Revenues	Sales Revenue	✓			
Revenues	Sales Revenue	✓			
Revenues	Sales Revenue	✓			
Revenues	Sales Revenue	✓			
Revenues	Sales Revenue	✓			

Step 3: Run Simulation.
Simulation Options
● Simulate All Options At Once
○ Simulate Selected Option Only
Simulation Trials   100
☑ Apply Seed Value   123
Defaults...   Correlations...   Run Simulation

Step 4: Save/Edit Simulation Models
Name: All Simulations Model All Assumptions
New
Save As
Edit
Save
Delete

Model
All Simulations Model All Assumptions
Project 1 Simulation

Assumption Properties

Triangular   Normal   Uniform
Arcsine   Bernoulli   Beta
Beta 3   Beta 4   Binomial
Cauchy   Chi-Square   Cosine

Minimum   5,868.5700
Most Likely   11,737.1400
Maximum   17,605.7100

OK   Cancel
Delete Assumption
Set Simulation Assumptions for Multiple Years

Triangular Distribution
The triangular distribution describes a situation where you know the minimum, maximum, and most likely values to occur. For example, you could describe the number of cars sold per week when past sales show the minimum, maximum, and usual number of cars sold. The minimum number of items is fixed, the maximum number of items is fixed, and the most likely number of items falls between the minimum and maximum values, forming a triangular-shaped distribution, which shows that values near the minimum and maximum are less likely to occur than those near the most-likely value. Minimum value (Min), most likely value (Likely) and maximum value (Max) are the distributional

Figure 5.1 – Risk Simulation: Set Input Assumptions

[EXAMPLE] - PROJECT ECONOMICS ANALYSIS TOOL

File Edit Projects Report Tools Language Decimals Help

Welcome to the ROV Project Economics Analysis Tool (PEAT). This module will help you set up a series of projects or Capital Investment Options, model their Cash Flows, Simulate Risks, and run Advanced Analytics; perform Forecasting and Prediction Modeling; and Optimize your Investment Portfolio subject to Budgetary and other Constraints.

Discounted Cash Flow   Applied Analytics   Risk Simulation   Overlay Results   Analysis of Alternatives   Dynamic Sensitivity

Set Input Assumptions   Simulation Results   Options Valuation   Forecast Prediction   Portfolio Optimization   Dashboard   Knowledge Center

Select the Option and Output Variable to view the results:

Project 1: Net Present Value (NPV)

Bar Type: Bar   Bar Color   Line Index: 1   Data Labels   Custom Text Properties   S-Curve Color

Project 1: Net Present Value (NPV)

Statistics/Percentile	Value
Trials	100
Mean	644,282.2281
Median	605,327.2369
Stdev	228,606.4373
CV	35.4823%
Skew	0.5845
Kurtosis	0.1540
Minimum	211,990.0629
Maximum	1,337,702.3254
Range	1,125,712.2624
0%	211,990.0629
5%	321,831.2036
10%	354,252.1257
20%	486,283.2629
30%	527,827.3614
40%	564,521.6910
50%	605,327.2369

Name: NPV Project 1 - 90% Confidence

Model
NPV Project 1 - 90% Confidence
NPV Project 2 - 90% Confidence
IRR Project 3 - 90% Confidence
NPV Project 3 - Probability NPV > 0

New   Save As   Edit   Save   Delete

☑ When saving, include simulated data and results (this may result in slower response and larger file sizes)

4   Decimals

Open   Save

Show vertical lines at: PDF Histogram   Update   Compute and Show lines at: Two Tails

Percentiles %:   Show Gridlines   Percentiles: 5   %   95   %

Certainty Values: 500,000.00   Value: 321,831.20   1,041,419.28

Copy Chart   Extract Simulation Data

Target Value

0.00 211,990.06   437,132.52   662,274.97   887,417.42   1,112,559.87   1,337,702.33

Frequency

14.00   12.00   10.00   8.00   6.00   4.00   2.00   0.00

Figure 5.2 – Risk Simulation: Simulation Results

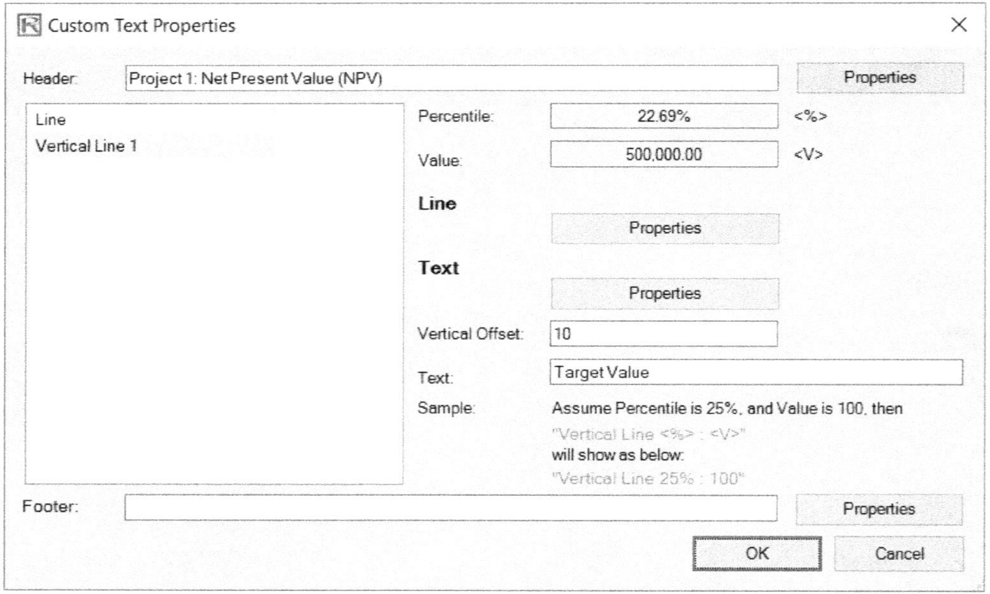

Custom Text Properties

Header:	Project 1: Net Present Value (NPV)	Properties

Line
Vertical Line 1

Percentile: 22.69% <%>

Value: 500,000.00 <V>

Line Properties

Text Properties

Vertical Offset: 10

Text: TargetValue

Sample: Assume Percentile is 25%, and Value is 100, then

"Vertical Line <%> : <V>"
will show as below.

"Vertical Line 25% : 100"

Properties

OK   Cancel

Footer:

Figure 5.3 – Risk Simulation: Custom Text

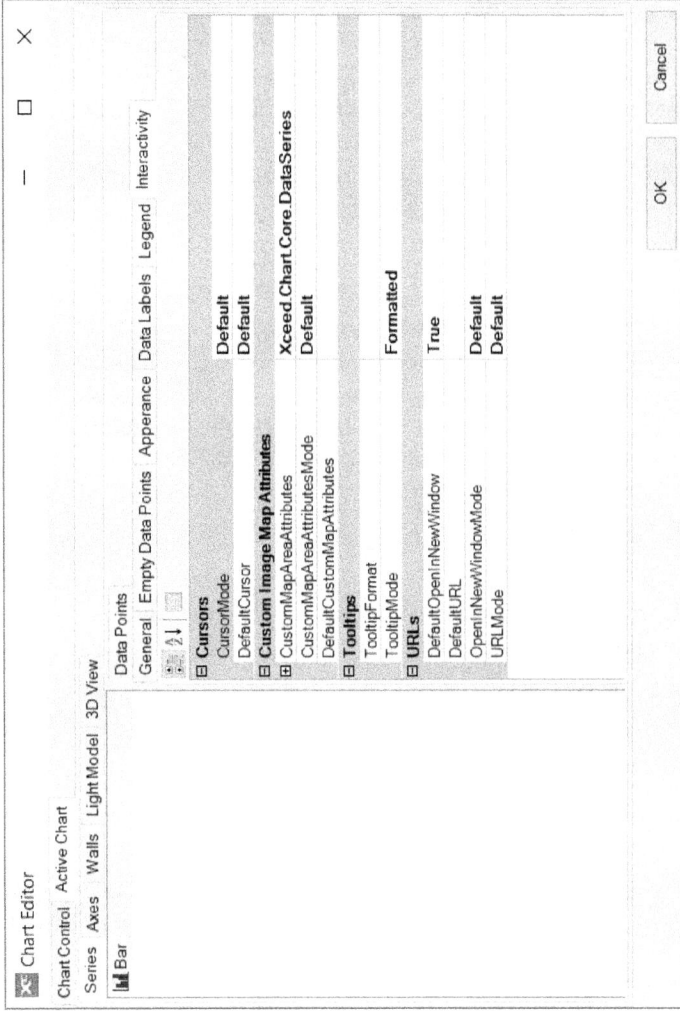

Figure 5.4 – Risk Simulation: Customizing Simulation Forecast Charts

Multiple simulation output variables can be compared at once using the *Overlay Results* tab (Figure 5.5 shows the DCF module's default example's results after running the Simulate All Options at Once selection, and then going to the Overlay Results, choosing the first two Project's NPV and selecting PDF Curve Overlay). Simply check/uncheck the simulated outputs you wish to compare and select the chart type to show (e.g., S-Curves, CDF, PDF). You can also add *Percentile* or *Certainty* lines by first selecting the output chart, entering the relevant values, and clicking the *Update* button. As usual, the generated charts are highly flexible in that you can modify the charts using the included chart icons. Some additional tips include:

- Typically, S-curves (CDF) curves are used in overlay analysis, when comparing the risk profile of multiple simulated forecast results. You can also change the chart into a PDF curve (see Figure 5.5) to see how one project stacks up against another (with central tendencies showing the expected returns, the width showing the potential uncertainties and risks, the directional skewness of each project, the excess fatness in the tails or peakedness in the distribution, etc.).

- Note that the more simulation trials you run, the smoother the chart looks. Figure 5.5 shows only a 100-trial run to illustrate, hence the jagged line charts.

- Refer to the Dr. Johnathan Mun's *Modeling Risk, Third Edition*, for more details on interpreting forecast distribution charts, statistical moments in the forecast charts, S-curves, PDFs, CDFs, and other associated charts.

- You can also view the *Basics of Project Economics Analysis* in the *Knowledge Center* for quick details on interpreting S-curves.

Risk Simulation | Analysis of Alternatives

While the *Overlay Results* show the simulated results as charts (PDF/CDF), the *Analysis of Alternatives* tab (Figure 5.6 shows the DCF module's default example's risk simulation Analysis of Alternatives results after running the All Simulations Model) shows the results of the simulation statistics in a table format as well as a chart of the statistics such that one Project can be compared against another. The default is to run an *Analysis of Alternatives* to compare one Project versus another, but you can also choose the *Incremental Analysis* project (remember to choose the *Base Case* to compare the results to). For instance, Figure 5.6 shows the relative coefficient of variation (a proxy for project volatility and relative risks) for all projects compared side by side.

Risk Simulation | Dynamic Sensitivity

Tornado analysis and Scenario analysis are both static calculations. *Dynamic Sensitivity* (Figure 5.7 shows the DCF module's default example's Dynamic Sensitivity results after running the Simulate All Options at Once), in contrast, is a dynamic analysis, which can only be performed after a simulation is run. While tornado analysis applies static perturbations before a simulation run, sensitivity analysis applies dynamic perturbations created after the simulation run. Tornado and spider charts are the results of static perturbations, meaning that each precedent or assumption variable is perturbed a preset amount one at a time, and the fluctuations in the results are tabulated. In contrast, sensitivity charts are the results of dynamic perturbations in the sense that multiple assumptions are perturbed simultaneously and their interactions in the model and correlations among variables are captured in the fluctuations of the results. Tornado charts therefore identify which variables drive the results the most and hence are suitable for simulation, whereas sensitivity charts identify the impact on the results when multiple interacting variables are simulated together in the model. A tornado chart's presimulation critical success factors will therefore sometimes be different from a sensitivity chart's post-simulation critical success factor. The post-simulation critical success factors should be the ones that are of interest as these more readily capture the model precedents' interactions.

Red bars on the *Rank Correlation* chart indicate negative correlations and green bars indicate positive correlations for the left chart. The correlations' absolute values are used to rank the variables with the highest relationship to the lowest, for all simulation input assumptions. *Contribution to Variance* indicates the percentage fluctuation in the output variable that can be statistically explained by the fluctuations in each of the input variables.

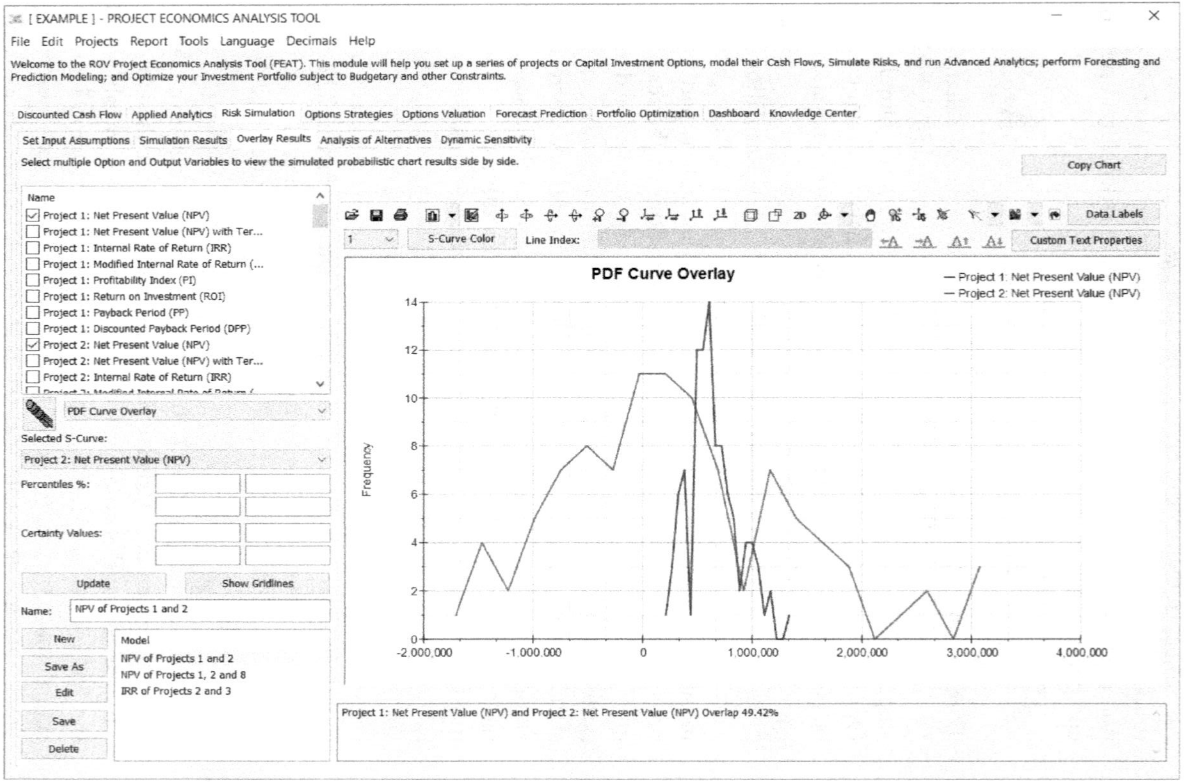

Figure 5.5 – Risk Simulation: Overlay Results

Welcome to the ROV Project Economics Analysis Tool (PEAT). This module will help you set up a series of projects or Capital Investment Options, model their Cash Flows, Simulate Risks, and run Advanced Analytics; perform Forecasting and Prediction Modeling; and Optimize your Investment Portfolio subject to Budgetary and other Constraints.

Discounted Cash Flow   Applied Analytics   Risk Simulation   Simulation Results   Overlay Results   Analysis of Alternatives   Options Valuation   Forecast Prediction   Portfolio Optimization   Dashboard   Knowledge Center

Set Input Assumptions   Simulation Results   Analysis of Alternatives   Dynamic Sensitivity

You can compare the dynamic simulated results of all your options. A simulation must first be run before you can obtain any results. Choose if you wish to compare all options as standalone (Analysis of Alternatives) or against a base case (Incremental Analysis).

ANALYSIS OF ALTERNATIVES AND BASE CASE INCREMENTAL ANALYSIS

◉ Analysis of Alternatives (No Base Case)   ○ Incremental Analysis (Choose Base Case):

Analysis of Alternatives: Net Present Value (NPV)

Economic Results: Net Present Value (NPV)

OPTIONS	Project 1	Project 2	Project 3	Project 4	Project 5	Project 6	Project 7	Project :
◉ Mean	644,282.23	301,497.52	31,569.79	34,258.97	97,218.08	72,431.35	1,166,523.85	434,249.4
○ Median	605,327.24	197,050.28	31,521.06	32,677.96	99,109.99	69,428.39	993,708.96	415,209.
○ Stdev	228,606.44	1,058,508.23	26,061.79	23,961.79	32,925.33	23,814.89	1,845,581.81	509,178.
○ Variance	5.17E-010	1.11E+012	6.72E+008	5.68E+008	1.07E+009	5.61E+008	3.37E+012	2.57E+01
○ CV	35.48%	351.08%	82.55%	69.94%	33.87%	32.86%	158.21%	117.25%
○ Skew	0.5845	0.6090	0.4384	0.3650	-0.0494	0.7115	0.4933	0.5029
○ Kurtosis	0.1540	0.1750	0.0616	-0.1492	0.0364	0.9877	0.1521	0.0669
○ Minimum	211,990.06	-1,704,332.28	-22,769.39	-18,288.92	10,923.44	24,528.81	-2,228,649.68	-536,796.
○ Maximum	1,337,702.33	3,075,908.86	104,572.94	91,719.62	176,995.11	160,545.23	6,713,638.76	1,969,898.
○ Range	1,125,712.26	4,780,241.14	127,342.34	110,008.54	166,071.67	136,016.42	8,942,288.44	2,506,695.
○ 0% Percentile	211,990.06	-1,704,332.28	-22,769.39	-18,288.92	10,923.44	24,528.81	-2,228,649.68	-536,796.
○ 5% Percentile	321,831.20	-1,345,042.67	9,092.02	-696.95	42,235.97	39,152.55	-1,588,929.86	-290,492.
○ 10% Percentile	354,252.13	-894,217.14	-402.59	3,904.81	56,297.95	43,646.51	-918,471.49	-186,857.
○ 20% Percentile	486,283.26	-543,560.75	10,549.18	14,433.90	69,554.67	52,498.52	-537,810.74	-37,188.0
○ 30% Percentile	527,827.36	-321,578.64	16,989.66	21,414.17	79,473.86	61,376.32	-31,247.05	130,122.
○ 40% Percentile	564,521.89	-100,719.80	24,419.90	26,983.10	89,003.88	64,908.03	569,148.95	236,954.
○ 50% Percentile	605,327.24	197,050.28	31,521.06	32,677.96	99,109.99	69,428.39	993,708.96	415,209.
○ 60% Percentile	649,850.43	449,243.73	35,943.52	40,052.59	107,337.63	74,955.59	1,445,004.68	516,294.
○ 70% Percentile	742,290.52	630,730.72	42,252.41	44,035.03	112,878.49	81,353.10	2,021,748.10	685,250.
○ 80% Percentile	839,307.57	1,166,093.19	51,192.45	50,698.03	124,145.74	91,784.97	2,658,639.27	846,002.
○ 90% Percentile	981,401.91	1,599,787.79	70,407.68	72,397.88	137,358.47	102,569.21	3,759,013.22	1,096,233.
○ 95% Percentile	1,041,419.28	2,478,189.35	78,244.81	79,104.03	144,455.41	112,206.00	4,330,837.14	1,314,070.
○ 100% Percentile	1,337,702.33	3,075,908.86	104,572.94	91,719.62	176,995.11	160,545.23	6,713,638.76	1,969,898.

Project 1   2 ⬍ Decimals

Net Present Value (NPV) (Options)

Options

2D Bar   Copy Chart

Figure 5.6 – Risk Simulation: Analysis of Alternatives

Figure 5.7 – Risk Simulation: Dynamic Sensitivity

EXAMPLE - PROJECT ECONOMICS ANALYSIS TOOL

File Edit Projects Report Tools Language Decimals Help

Welcome to the ROV Project Economics Analysis Tool (PEAT). This module will help you set up a series of projects or Capital Investment Options, model their Cash Flows, Simulate Risks, and run Advanced Analytics; perform Forecasting and Prediction Modeling; and Optimize your Investment Portfolio subject to Budgetary and other Constraints.

Discounted Cash Flow   Applied Analytics   Risk Simulation   Options Strategies   Options Valuation   Forecast Prediction   Portfolio Optimization   Dashboard   Knowledge Center

Set Input Assumptions   Simulation Results   Overlay Results   Analysis of Alternatives   Dynamic Sensitivity

Dynamic Sensitivity is run by first performing a Monte Carlo Risk Simulation to model its dynamic interactions and impacts on the selected output variables. To get started, make sure you have a simulation already run, then choose the Option and Output Variable you wish to test and click Compute to run the analysis.

Select the Option and Output Variable to run:

Project 1: Internal Rate of Return (IRR)

Show 15 Rows

Name: IRR Project 1

New
Save As
Edit
Save
Delete

Copy Charts

Model
NPV Project 1
NPV Project 2
IRR Project 1

Project 1: Internal Rate of Return (IRR)

Nonlinear Rank Correlation

DCF | CAPITAL INVESTMENTS | 2016   -0.90
Revenues | Sales Revenue - Global Sale   0.37
Direct Costs | Fabrication | 2033   0.90
Indirect Expenses | Sales and Administ -0.27
Direct Costs | Direct R&D | 2036   0.25
Indirect Expenses | Channel Partners   -0.25
Indirect Expenses | Channel Partners   0.45
CFR | Stock Price Per Share   -0.25
DCF | Marginal Tax Rate (%)   -0.24
Direct Costs | Direct R&D | 2031   0.24
Direct Costs | Direct COGS | 2032   -0.23
Indirect Expenses | Operations | 2039   -0.22
Revenues | Sales Revenue - Global Sale -0.22
Direct Costs | Direct R&D | 2023   -0.21
Direct Costs | Direct R&D | 2024   0.21

0 0.1 0.2 0.3 0.4 0.5 0.6 0.7 0.8

Contribution to Variance

4.54%
3.15%
2.02%
1.66%
1.48%
1.47%
1.45%
1.41%
1.35%
1.28%
1.25%
1.14%
1.08%
1.03%
0.99%

0 0.02 0.04 0.06 0.08 0.1 0.12 0.14 0.16

STRATEGIC OPTIONS

Options Strategies is where you can draw your own custom strategic map or strategic real options paths (Figure 6.1). This section only allows you to draw and visualize these strategic pathways and does not perform any computations. The next section, *Options Valuation,* actually does the computations. Feel free to explore this section's capabilities but we recommend viewing the *Video on Options Strategies* (in the *Knowledge Center | Getting Started Videos* section of the software) to quickly get started on using this very powerful tool. You can also explore some preset options strategies by clicking on the *First Icon* and selecting any one of the *Examples.*

The default methodology shown is that of a Strategy Tree (i.e., only visual representations of strategic implementation pathways of investments with no computations performed; all quantitative computations and valuations are performed in the next tab, *Options Valuation*). Simulated dynamic decision trees are also available by clicking on the *ROV Decision Trees* button or the *Last Icon* (decision trees can be used to perform basic decision models as well as other more advanced methods like risk simulation on decision nodes, Bayes' theorem applications and Bayes' updating, expected value of information, utility functions analysis, and so forth). Below are some notes on the elements you will encounter in the software:

- *Insert Option* nodes or *Insert Terminal* nodes by first selecting any existing node and then clicking on the option node icon (square) or terminal node icon (triangle).

- Modify individual *Option Node* or *Terminal Node* properties by double-clicking on a node. Sometimes when you click on a node, all subsequent child nodes are also selected (this allows you to move the entire tree starting from that selected node). If you wish to select only that node, you may have to click on the empty background and click back on that node to select it individually. Also, you can move individual nodes or the entire tree starting from the selected node depending on the current setting (right-click, or in the *Edit* menu, and select *Move Nodes Individually* or *Move Nodes Together*).

- The following are some quick descriptions of the things that can be customized and configured in the node properties user interface. It is simplest to try different settings for each of the following to see its effects in the Strategy Tree:

  o *Name.* Name shown above the node.

  o *Value.* Value shown below the node.

  o *Excel Link.* Links the value from an Excel spread-sheet's cell.

  o *Notes.* Notes can be inserted above or below a node.

  o *Show in Model.* Show any combinations of Name, Value, and Notes.

  o *Local Color* versus *Global Color.* Node colors can be changed locally to a node or globally.

  o *Label Inside Shape.* Text can be placed inside the node (you may need to make the node wider to accommo-date longer text).

  o *Branch Event Name.* Text can be placed on the branch leading to the node to indicate the event leading to this node.

  o *Select Real Options.* A specific real option type can be assigned to the current node. Assigning real options to nodes allows the tool to generate a list of required input variables.

- *Global Elements* are all customizable, including elements of the Strategy Tree's *Background, Connection Lines, Option Nodes, Terminal Nodes,* and *Text Boxes.* For instance, the following settings can be changed for each of the elements:

  o *Font* settings on Name, Value, Notes, Label, Event names.

  o *Node Size* (minimum and maximum height and width).

- o *Borders* (line styles, width, and color).
- o *Shadow* (colors and whether to apply a shadow or not).
- o *Global Color.*
- o *Global Shape.*

- *Example Files* are available in the *first icon* menu to help you get started on building Strategy Trees.

- *Protect File* from the *first icon* menu allows the Strategy Tree to be encrypted with up to a 256-bit password encryption. Be careful when a file is being encrypted because if the password is lost, the file can no longer be opened.

- *Capturing the Screen* or printing the existing model can be done through the *first icon* menu. The captured screen can then be pasted into other software applications.

- *Add, Duplicate, Rename,* and *Delete a Strategy Tree* can be performed through right-clicking the Strategy Tree tab or the *Edit* menu.

- You can also *Insert File Link* and *Insert Comment* on any option or terminal node or *Insert Text* or *Insert Picture* anywhere in the background or canvas area.

- You can *Change Existing Styles* or *Manage and Create Custom Styles* of your Strategy Tree (this includes size, shape, color schemes, and font size/color specifications of the entire Strategy Tree).

Options Valuation

The *Options Valuation* section performs the calculations of Real Options Valuation models (Figures 6.2–6.5 show the results of using the default load example inputs). Make sure you understand the basic concepts of real options before proceeding. Briefly, start by choosing the *option execution type* (e.g., American, Bermudan, or European), select an option to model (e.g., single phased and single asset or multiple phased sequential options), and, based on the option types selected, enter the required inputs and click *Compute*. Some basic information and a sample strategic path are shown on the right under *Strategy View*. Also, a *Tornado* analysis and *Scenario* analysis can be performed on the option model, and you can *Save As* the options models for future retrieval.

You can click on *Load Example* to load an example set of inputs you can use as a guide to implementing your own option model, or click on the *Manual Input* droplists to automatically compute the inputs based on the projects you selected (i.e., some of the real options inputs will be linked to and computed from the outputs of the DCF model and simulation results).

Options Execution Types

- *American Options* can be executed at any time up to and including the maturity date.

- *European Options* can be executed only at one point in time, the maturity date.

- *Bermudan Options* can be executed at certain times and can be considered a hybrid of American and European Options. There is typically a blackout or vesting period when the option cannot be executed; but starting from the end of the blackout vesting date to the option's maturity, the option can be executed.

Option to Wait and Execute

Buy additional time to wait for new information by pre-negotiating pricing and other contractual terms to obtain the option but not the obligation to purchase or execute something in the future should conditions warrant it (wait and see before executing).

- Run a Proof of Concept first to better determine the costs and schedule risks of a project versus jumping in right now and taking the risk.

- Build, Buy, or Lease. Developing internally or using commercially available technology or products.

- Multiple Contracts in place that may or not be executed.

- Market Research to obtain valuable information before deciding.

- Venture Capital small seed investment with right of first refusal before executing large-scale financing.

- Relative values of Strategic Analysis of Alternatives or Courses of Action while considering risk and the Value of Information.

- Contract Negotiations with vendors, acquisition strategy with industrial-based ramifications (competitive sustainment and strategic capability and availability).

- Project Evaluation and Capability ROI modeling.

- Capitalizing on other opportunities while reducing large-scale implementation risks and determining the value of Research & Development (parallel implementation of alternatives while waiting on technical success of the main project, and no need to delay the project because of one bad component in the project).

- Low Rate Initial Production, Prototyping, and Advanced Concept Technology Demonstration before full-scale implementation.

- Right of First Refusal contracts.

- Value of Information by forecasting cost inputs, capability, schedule, and other metrics.

- Hedging and Call- and Put-like options to execute something in the future with agreed upon terms now, OTC Derivatives (Price, Demand, Forex, Interest Rate forwards, futures, options, swaptions for hedging).

Option to Abandon

Hedge downside risks and losses by being able to salvage some value of a failed project or asset that is out-of-the-money (sell intellectual property and assets, abandon and walk away from a project, buyback/sellback provisions).

- Exit and Salvage assets and intellectual property to reduce losses.

- Divestiture and Spin-off.

- Buyback Provisions in a contract.

- Stop and Abandon before executing the next phase.

- Termination for Convenience.

- Early Exit and Stop Loss Provisions in a contract.

Option to Expand

Take advantage of upside opportunities by having existing platform, structure, or technology that can be readily expanded (utility peaking plants, larger oil platforms, early/leapfrog technology development, larger capacity or technology-in-place for future expansion).

- Platform Technologies.

- Mergers and Acquisitions.

- Built-in Expansion Capabilities.

- Geographical, Technological, and Market Expansion.

- Foreign Military Sales.

- Reusability and Scalability.

Option to Contract

Reduce downside risk but still participate in reduced benefits (counterparty takes over or joins in some activities to share profits; at the same time reduce your firm's risk of failure or severe losses in a risky but potentially profitable venture).

- Outsourcing, Alliances, Contractors, Leasing.

- Joint Venture.

- Foreign Partnerships.

- Co-Development and Co-Marketing.

Portfolio Options

Combinations of options and strategic flexibility within a portfolio of nested options (path dependencies, mutually exclusive/inclusive, nested options).

- Determining the portfolio of projects' capabilities to develop and field within Budget and Time Constraints, and what new Product Configurations to develop or acquire to field certain capabilities.

- Allows for different Flexible Pathways: Mutually Exclusive (P1 or P2 but not both), Platform/Prerequisite Technology (P3 requires P2, but P2 can be stand-alone; expensive and worth less if considered by itself without accounting for flexibility downstream options it provides for in the next phase), expansion options, abandonment options, parallel development or simultaneous compound options.

- Determining the Optimal Portfolios given budget scenarios that provide the maximum capability, flexibility, and cost effectiveness with minimal risks.

- Determining testing required in Modular Systems, mean-time-to-failure estimates, and Replacement and Redundancy requirements.

- Relative value of strategic Flexibility Options (options to Abandon, Choose, Contract, Expand, and Switch, and Sequential Compound Options, Barrier Options, and many other types of Exotic Options).

- Maintaining Capability and Readiness Levels.

- Product Mix, Inventory Mix, Production Mix.

- Capability Selection and Sourcing.

Sequential Options

Significant value exists if you can phase out investments over time, thereby reducing the risk of a one-time up-front investment (pharmaceutical and high technology development and manufacturing usually comes in phases or stages).

- Stage-gate implementation of high-risk project development, prototyping, low-rate-initial-production, technical feasibility tests, technology demonstration competitions.

- Government contracts with multiple stages with the option to abandon at any time and valuing Termination for Convenience, and built-in flexibility to execute different courses of action at specific stages of development.

- P3I, Milestones, R&D, and Phased Options.
- Platform technology.

Options to Switch

Ability to choose among several options, thereby improving strategic flexibility to maneuver within the realm of uncertainty (maintain a foot in one door while exploring another to decide if it makes sense to switch or stay put).

- Ability to Switch among various raw input materials to use when prices of each raw material fluctuates significantly.

- Readiness and capability risk mitigation through switching vendors in an Open Architecture through Multiple Vendors and Modular Design.

Other Types of Real Options

Barrier Options, Custom Options, Exotic Options, Simultaneous Compound Option, Employee Stock Options, Options Embedded Contracts, Options with Blackout/Vesting Provisions, Options with Market and Change of Control Provisions, and many others!

Options Input Assumptions

- *Asset Value.* The underlying asset value before implementation costs. You can compute it by taking the NPV and adding back the sum of the present values of capital investments.

- *Implementation Cost.* The cost to execute the option (typically this is the cost to execute an option to wait or an option to expand).

- *Volatility.* The annualized volatility (a measure of risk and uncertainty, in percent) of the underlying asset.

- *Maturity.* The maturity of the option, denoted in years (e.g., a two-and-a-half-year option life can be entered as 2.5).

- *Risk-free Rate.* The interest-rate yield on a risk-free government bond with maturity commensurate to that of the option.

- *Dividend Rate.* The annualized opportunity cost of not executing the option, as a percentage of the underlying asset.

- *Lattice Steps.* The number of binomial or multinomial lattice steps to run in the model. The typical number we recommend is between 100 and 1000, and you can check for convergence of the results. The larger the number of lattice steps, the higher the level of convergence and granularity (i.e., the number of decimal precision).

- *Blackout Year.* The vesting period entered in years, during which the option cannot be executed (European), but the option converts to an American on the date of this vesting period through to its maturity.

- *Maturity of Phases.* The number of years to the end of each phase in a sequential compound option model.

- *Cost to Implement Phases.* The costs to execute each of the subsequent phases in a sequential compound option, and they can be set to zero or a positive value.

- *Expansion Factor.* The relative ratio increase in the underlying asset when the option to expand is executed (typically this is greater than 1).

- *Contraction Factor.* The relative ratio reduction in the underlying asset when the option to contract is executed (typically this is less than 1).

- *Savings.* The net savings received by contracting operations.

- *Salvage.* The net sales amount after expenses of abandoning an asset.

- *Barrier.* The upper or lower barrier of an option whereupon if the underlying asset breaches this barrier, the option becomes either live or worthless, depending on the type of option modeled.

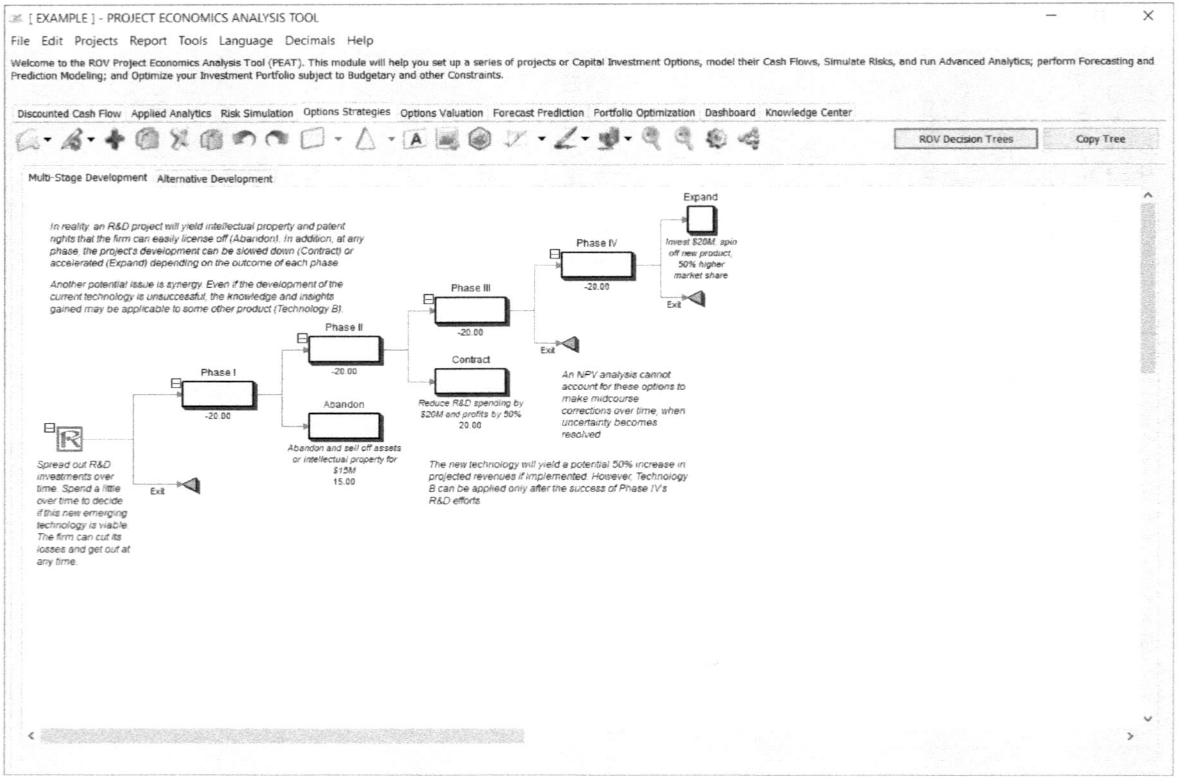

Figure 6.1 – Options Strategies

File   Edit   Projects   Report   Tools   Language   Decimals   Help

Welcome to the ROV Project Economics Analysis Tool (PEAT). This module will help you set up a series of projects or Capital Investment Options, model their Cash Flows, Simulate Risks, and run Advanced Analytics; perform Forecasting and Prediction Modeling; and Optimize your Investment Portfolio subject to Budgetary and other Constraints.

Discounted Cash Flow   Applied Analytics   Risk Simulation   Options Valuation   Forecast Prediction   Portfolio Optimization   Dashboard   Knowledge Center

Step 1: Select the option execution type:

This tab allows you to model and value the most common real options strategies. For more complex real options models (e.g., changing inputs over time, simulated inputs, complex customized options, nested options, et cetera), please use the Real Options SLS software instead.

( ) American   ( ) Bermudan   ( ) European

Step 2: Select the type of real options to model and value:

( ) Single Phased and Single Asset Options:

Step 5: Compute the strategic real options value:

Option to Abandon

[Compute]   Result: 450,355.4407

( ) Multiple Phased Sequential Options:

2 Phased Option (Proof of Concept, R&D)

Strategy View   Sensitivity   Tornado   Scenario

Step 3: Enter the real options input assumptions:

[Load Example]

Basic Option Assumptions:

Computes the value of an option to abandon. That is, you can exit the project and salvage the asset's or project's intellectual property to reduce further losses, stop before executing the next phase, or execute a termination for convenience while at the same time recovering some value. Remember that you can only execute an option to abandon if you already own the asset or project, otherwise please use the Option to Wait and Defer if you are just exiting a project without further execution. Enter a net salvage value after expenses of the amount that can be recovered at time of abandonment. In this option, the implementation cost is not used (you can enter any placeholder value as an input).

Asset Value (Present Value of Net Benefits):   445,625.18   [Manual Input]

Volatility (Annualized Risk %):   22.33%   [Manual Input]

Maturity (Total Years to Option Expiration):   5.00

Risk-Free Rate (Riskless Discount Rate %):   3.50%

Dividend Rate (Opportunity Cost %):   0.00%

Lattice Steps (Typically 100 to 1000):   100

Additional Single Phased Option Assumptions:

Salvage: 250,000.00

Step 4: Save/Edit Model (Optional):

Model Name:

Project 1 Abandonment Option

Model

Project 1 Abandonment Option
Project 3 Expansion Option
Project 8 Two Phased Investment

[Save As...]   [Edit]

[Delete]   [Save]

Continue with development

Project

Abandon

Abandon the project and sell
the project's asset or
intellectual property and
obtain some salvage value

Figure 6.2 – Options Valuation: Input Assumptions and Strategy View

File Edit Projects Report Tools Language Decimals Help

Welcome to the ROV Project Economics Analysis Tool (PEAT). This module will help you set up a series of projects or Capital Investment Options, model their Cash Flows, Simulate Risks, and run Advanced Analytics; perform Forecasting and Prediction Modeling; and Optimize your Investment Portfolio subject to Budgetary and other Constraints.

Discounted Cash Flow Applied Analytics Risk Simulation Options Strategies Options Valuation Forecast Prediction Portfolio Optimization Dashboard Knowledge Center

Step 1: Select the option execution type:

This tab allows you to model and value the most common real options strategies. For more complex real options models (e.g., changing inputs over time, simulated inputs, complex customized options, nested options, et cetera), please use the Real Options SLS software instead.

○ American   ○ Bermudan   ○ European

Step 2: Select the type of real options to model and value:

○ Single Phased and Single Asset Options:
   Option to Abandon

● Multiple Phased Sequential Options:
   2 Phased Option (Proof of Concept, R&D)
   [Phased Option (Proof of Concept, R&D)]
   3 Phased Option (Phased Development)
   Beta 4 Phased Option (Phased Development)
   5 Phased Option (Phased Development)
   At Complex 2 Phased Option (Abandon, Contract, Expand)   Manual Input

Load Example
al Input

Step 5: Compute the strategic real options value:

Compute   Result: 450,355.4407

Strategy View Sensitivity Tornado Scenario

Sensitivity +/-   10 ◄► %
Show the top   10 ◄► variables
Show results with   2 ◄► decimals

Update   Copy Grid

Volatility (Annualized Risk %):   22.33%

Risk-Free Rate (Riskless Discount Rate %):   3.50%
Dividend Rate (Opportunity Cost %):   0.00%
Lattice Steps (Typically 100 to 1000):   100

Additional Multiple Phased Option Assumptions:
Maturity of Phase 1:   Cost to Implement Phase 1:
Maturity of Phase 2:   Cost to Implement Phase 2:

Step 4: Save/Edit Model (Optional):
Model Name:
Project 1 Abandonment Option

Save As...   Edit
Delete   Save

Model
Project 1 Abandonment Option
Project 3 Expansion Option
Project 8 Two Phased Investment

American::Option to Abandon

Base Value: 450,355...

Inputs	Output Downside	Output Upside	Effective Range	Input Changes Downside	Input Changes Upside	Base Case Value
Asset Value (Present Value of Net Be...	408,303...	493,322...	85,018.53	401,062...	490,187...	445,625...
Salvage	448,310...	453,264...	4,954.40	225,000...	275,000...	250,000...
Volatility (Annualized Risk %)	448,529...	452,617...	4,087.47	20.10%	24.56%	22.33%
Maturity (Total Years to Option Expi...	449,638...	451,034...	1,395.74	4.50	5.50	5.00
Risk-Free Rate (Riskless Discount Ra...	450,726...	450,009...	716.96	3.15%	3.85%	3.50%
Lattice Steps (Typically 100 to 1000)	450,372...	450,314...	58.01	90.00	110.00	100.00
Dividend Rate (Opportunity Cost %)	450,355...	450,355...	0.00	0.00%	0.00%	0.00%

Figure 6.3 – Options Valuation: Sensitivity Analysis on Options

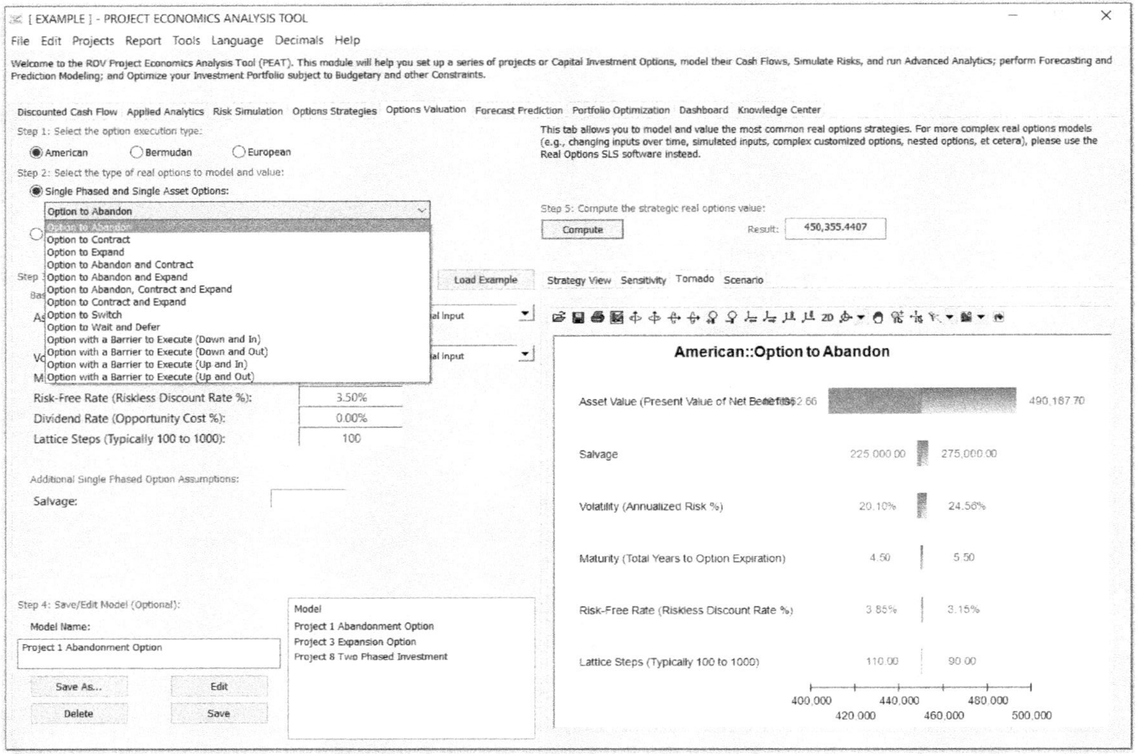

Figure 6.4 – Options Valuation: Tornado Analysis on Options

File   Edit   Projects   Report   Tools   Language   Decimals   Help

Welcome to the ROV Project Economics Analysis Tool (PEAT). This module will help you set up a series of projects or Capital Investment Options, model their Cash Flows, Simulate Risks, and run Advanced Analytics; perform Forecasting and Prediction Modeling; and Optimize your Investment Portfolio subject to Budgetary and other Constraints.

Discounted Cash Flow   Applied Analytics   Risk Simulation   Options Valuation   Options Strategies   Forecast Prediction   Portfolio Optimization   Dashboard   Knowledge Center

This tab allows you to model and value the most common real options strategies. For more complex real options models (e.g., changing inputs over time, simulated inputs, complex customized options, nested options, et cetera), please use the Real Options SLS software instead.

Step 1: Select the option execution type:
( ) American   ( ) Bermudan   ( ) European

Step 2: Select the type of real options to model and value:
( ) Single Phased and Single Asset Options:
   Option to Abandon
( ) Multiple Phased Sequential Options:
   2 Phased Option (Proof of Concept, R&D)

Step 3: Enter the the real options input assumptions:

Basic Option Assumptions:

Asset Value (Present Value of Net Benefits):	445,625.18	Manual Input
Volatility (Annualized Risk %):	22.33%	Manual Input
Maturity (Total Years to Option Expiration):	3.50%	
Risk-Free Rate (Riskless Discount Rate %):	0.00%	
Dividend Rate (Opportunity Cost %):	100	
Lattice Steps (Typically 100 to 1000):		

Additional Single Phased Option Assumptions:
Salvage:

Step 4: Save/Edit Model (Optional):
Model Name:
Project 1 Abandonment Option

Model
Project 1 Abandonment Option
Project 3 Expansion Option
Project 8 Two Phased Investment

[Edit]   [Save]   [Save As...]   [Delete]

Step 5: Compute the strategic real options value:
[Compute]   Result: 450,355.4407

Strategy View   Sensitivity   Tornado   Scenario

Decimals: 2

Column Variable (Across):   Asset Value (Present Value of Net Benefits)
From 222,812.59   To 891,250.3   Step 111,406.3

Row Variable (Down):   Maturity (Total Years to Option Expiration)
From 2.50   To 10.00   Step 0.50

[Update Scenarios]   [Copy Grid]

	222,812.59	334,218.89	445,625.19	557,031.49	668,437.79	779,844.09	891,250.36
2.50	262,037.73	341,696.57	446,951.04	557,272.10	668,482.08	779,852.82	891,252.16
3.00	263,435.86	343,281.97	447,613.90	557,480.91	668,545.85	779,871.60	891,257.77
3.50	264,642.69	344,697.81	448,267.50	557,748.78	668,640.41	779,905.75	891,269.45
4.00	265,701.98	345,939.55	448,993.81	558,034.46	668,758.24	779,957.40	891,290.58
4.50	266,638.67	347,057.34	449,638.57	558,395.32	668,924.21	780,022.04	891,323.95
5.00	267,472.82	348,159.88	450,355.45	558,721.92	669,100.64	780,118.00	891,366.62
5.50	268,221.10	349,190.06	451,034.30	559,134.35	669,307.07	780,221.21	891,421.27
6.00	268,897.00	350,120.68	451,650.10	559,507.11	669,502.76	780,347.36	891,495.60
6.50	269,512.38	350,968.36	452,223.38	559,856.60	669,759.68	780,467.67	891,568.71
7.00	270,088.71	351,748.70	452,843.48	560,282.20	669,991.15	780,633.10	891,664.83
7.50	270,631.39	352,463.62	453,446.97	560,677.82	670,210.32	780,782.37	891,764.64
8.00	271,142.46	353,126.23	454,000.77	561,041.49	670,489.85	780,927.85	891,858.29
8.50	271,614.65	353,748.44	454,512.75	561,382.13	670,752.47	781,122.23	891,986.94

Figure 6.5 – Options Valuation: Scenario Analysis on Options

PEAT's Options Valuation tab is a simplified version of options analysis in the sense that the most common strategic real options have been incorporated into the software, and all you need to do is select the option you want valued, enter the required assumptions, and compute. The analysis is also backed by *Tornado Analysis*, *Sensitivity Analysis*, and *Scenario Analysis*. However, for more advanced or customized options, please use ROV's other software tool, Real Options Super Lattice Solver (SLS) as seen in Figure 6.6, where more advanced analytical models can be created (Figure 6.7).

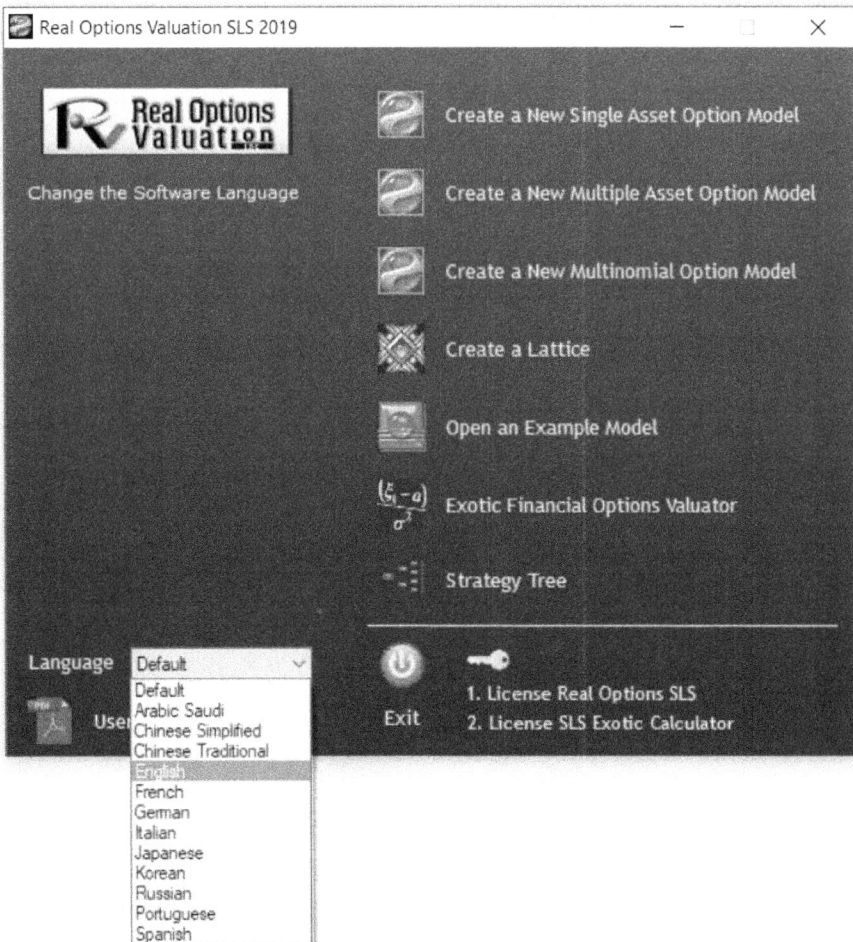

Figure 6.6 – Real Options Super Lattice Solver (SLS) Software

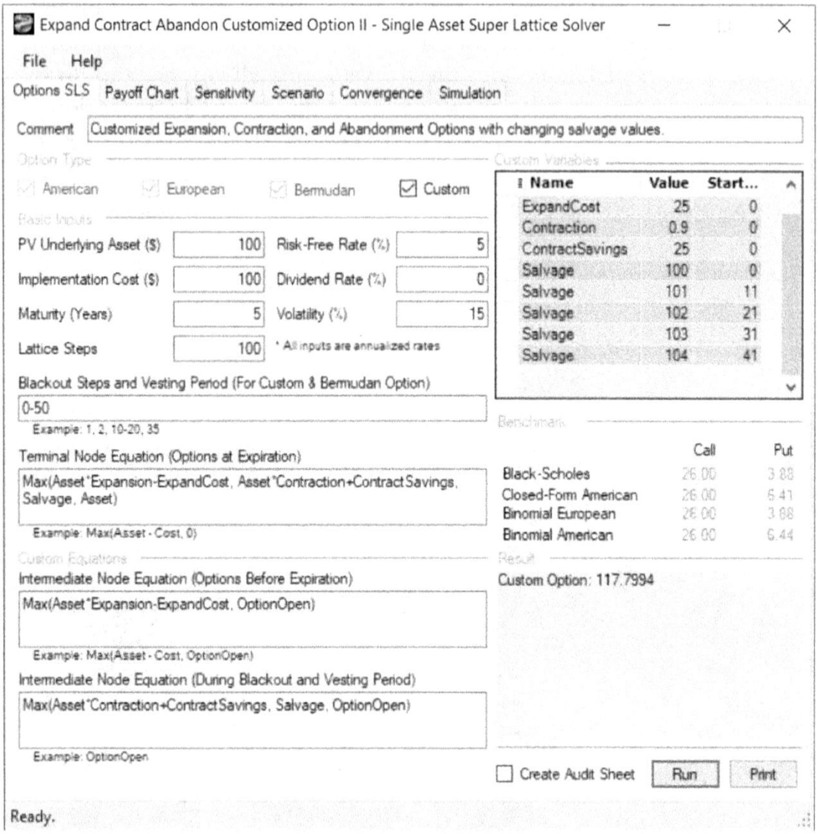

Figure 6.7 – Real Options Super Lattice Solver (SLS) Software: Sample Customized Option

FORECAST
PREDICTION

This section on *Forecast Prediction* (see Figures 7.1, 7.2, and 7.3) includes a sophisticated Business Analytics and Business Statistics module with over 250 functionalities. Start by entering the data in *Step 1* (copy and paste from Excel or other ODBC-compliant data source, manually type in data, or click on the *Options | Load Example* button to load a sample dataset complete with previously saved models). Then, choose the analysis to perform in *Step 2* and, using the variables list provided, enter the desired variables to model given the chosen analysis (if you previously clicked *Options | Load Example*, you can double-click to use and run the saved models in *Step 4* to see how variables are entered in *Step 2*, and use that as an example for your analysis). Click *RUN* in *Step 3* when ready to obtain the *Results, Charts,* and *Statistics* of the analysis. You can also *Save* your model in *Step 4* by giving it a name for future retrieval.

The following provides a few quick getting started steps on running the Forecast Prediction module and details on each of the elements in the software, and refer to Dr. Johnathan Mun's *Modeling Risk, Third Edition* with dedicated chapters explaining and exploring some of the most critical statistical methodologies available in this module. Feel free to explore the power of this Forecast Prediction module by loading the preset *Options | Load Example* or watch the Video to quickly get started using the module and review the user manual for more details on the 250 analytical methods. All 250 models are in ROV BizStats, while selected forecasting models are in this current PEAT software.

- Proceed to the Forecast Prediction tab and click on *Options | Load Example* to load a sample data and model profile or type in your data or copy/paste from another software such as Excel or Word/text file into the data grid in *Step 1* (Figure 7.1). You can add your own notes or variable names in the first *Notes* row.

- Select the relevant model to run in *Step 2* and using the example data input settings, enter in the relevant variables. Separate variables for the same parameter using semicolons and use a new line (hit *Enter* to create a new line) for different parameters.

- Click *Run* to compute the results. You can view any relevant analytical results, charts, or statistics from the various tabs in *Step 3*.

- If required, you can provide a model name to save into the profile in *Step 4*. Multiple models can be saved in the same profile. Existing models can be edited or deleted and rearranged in order of appearance, and all the changes can be saved.

- If you use your own data and create your own models, you can save these models in *Step 4*.

- If you are playing with the example data/models and need to recover your saved data and models, click on *Options | Recover My Models*.

- Saving your data and multiple models in *Step 4* will result in their being saved as part of the **rovprojecon* profile. In addition, if you click on *Options | Save/Open Profile,* you can save the data and models as a stand-alone **.bizstats* file that can be opened in a separate software, *ROV BizStats*.

TIPS on Using Forecast Prediction

- The data grid size can be set in the *Grid Configure* button, where the grid can accommodate up to 1,000 variable columns with 1 million rows of data per variable. The pop-up menu also allows you to change the language and decimal settings for your data.

- To get started, it is always a good idea to load the example file that comes complete with some data and precreated models. You can double-click on any of these models to run them and the results are shown in the report area, which sometimes can be a chart or model statistics. Using this example file, you can now see how the input parameters are entered based on the model description, and you can proceed to create your own custom models.

- Click on the variable headers to select one or multiple variables at once, and then right-click to add, delete, copy, paste, or visualize the variables selected.

- Models can also be entered using a *Command* console (Figure 7.3). To see how this works, double-click to run a model and go to the *Command* console. You can replicate the model or create your own and click *Run Command* when ready. Each line in the console represents a model and its relevant parameters.

- Click on the data grid's column header(s) to select the entire column(s) or variable(s), and once selected, you can right-click on the header to *Auto Fit* the column, or to *Cut, Copy, Delete,* or *Paste* data. You can also click on and select multiple column headers to select multiple variables and right-click and select *Visualize* to chart the data.

- If a cell has a large value that is not completely displayed, click on and hover your mouse over that cell and you will see a pop-up comment showing the entire value, or simply resize the variable column (drag the column to make it wider, double-click on the column's edge to auto fit the column, or right-click on the column header and select *Auto Fit*).

- Use the up, down, left, and right keys to move around the grid, or use the *Home* and *End* keys on the keyboard to move to the far left and far right of a row. You can also use combination keys such as *Ctrl+Home* to jump to the top left cell, *Ctrl+End* to the bottom right cell, *Shift+Up/Down* to select a specific area, and so forth.

- You can enter short notes for each variable in the *Notes* row.

- Try out the various chart icons on the *Visualize* tab to change the look and feel of the charts (e.g., rotate, shift, zoom, change colors, add legend, etc.).

- The *Copy* button is used to copy the *Results*, *Charts*, and *Statistics* tabs in *Step 3* after a model is run. If no models are run, then the *Copy* function will only copy a blank page.

- The *Report* button will only run if there are saved models in *Step 4* or if there are data in the grid, otherwise the report generated will be empty. You will also need Microsoft Excel to be installed to run the data extraction and results reports, and Microsoft PowerPoint available to run the chart reports.

- When in doubt about how to run a specific model or statistical method, start the *Options | Load Example* profile and review how the data is set up in *Step 1* or how the input parameters are entered in *Step 2*. You can use these as getting started guides and templates for your own data and models.

- Click the *Options | Load Example* button to load a sample set of previously saved data and models. Then double-click on one of the *Saved Models* in *Step 4*. You can see the saved model that is selected, and the input variables used in *Step 2*. The results will be computed and shown in the *Step 3* results area, and you can view the *Results*, *Charts*, or *Statistics* depending on what is available based on the model you chose and ran.

- The *Grid Configure* button allows you to change the number of rows or columns of the data grid in *Step 1*.

- Click *Report* only if you need it. That is, this function will run all of the saved models in *Step 4* and extract the results to Microsoft Excel, Word, and PowerPoint. We say do it only if you mean it because if you have too many saved models, it will run all models and the entire process might take a few minutes to complete.

- You can save a model if required after setting up the model (entering the data, selecting the model, and configuring the input parameters in *Step 2*) after you give it a *Name* in *Step 4* and click *Save*. You can *Edit* or *Delete* saved models later.

- You can copy data from another software, such as Microsoft Excel, and paste it into the data grid in *Step 1*. Simply copy the data, click on the location you wish the data to be pasted into, right-click, and select *Paste*.

- If your data contains large values (e.g., 10,000,000.00), right-click anywhere in the data grid and select *Auto Fit All Columns*.

- You can select a variable in the data grid by clicking on the header(s). For instance, you can click on *VAR1* and it will select the entire variable.

- When a variable is selected, click on the *Visualize* button or *right-click* and select *Visualize*, and the data will be collapsed into a time-series chart.

- Depending on the model run, sometimes the results will return a chart (e.g., a stochastic process forecast was created, and the results are presented both in the *Results* subtab and the *Charts* subtab).

- The charts subtab has multiple chart icons you can use to change the appearance of the chart (e.g., modify the chart type, chart line colors, chart view, etc.).

- Sometimes you can also quickly run multiple models using direct commands (e.g., using the *Command Console*.

- For new users, we recommend setting up the models using the user interface, starting from *Step 1* through to *Step 4*.

- To start using the console, create the models you need, then click on the *Command* subtab, copy/edit/replicate the command syntax (e.g., you can replicate a model multiple times and change some of its input parameters very quickly using the command approach), and when ready, click on the *Run Command* button.

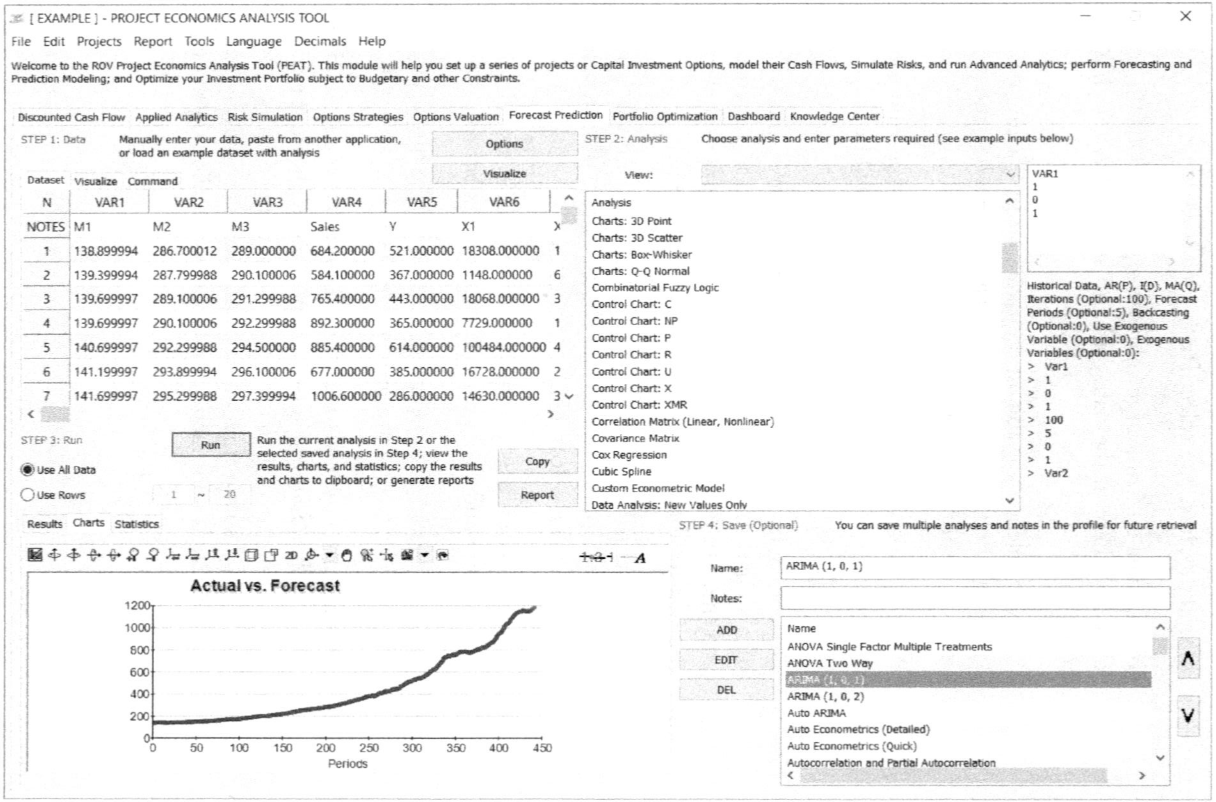

Figure 7.1 – Forecast Prediction: Module Overview

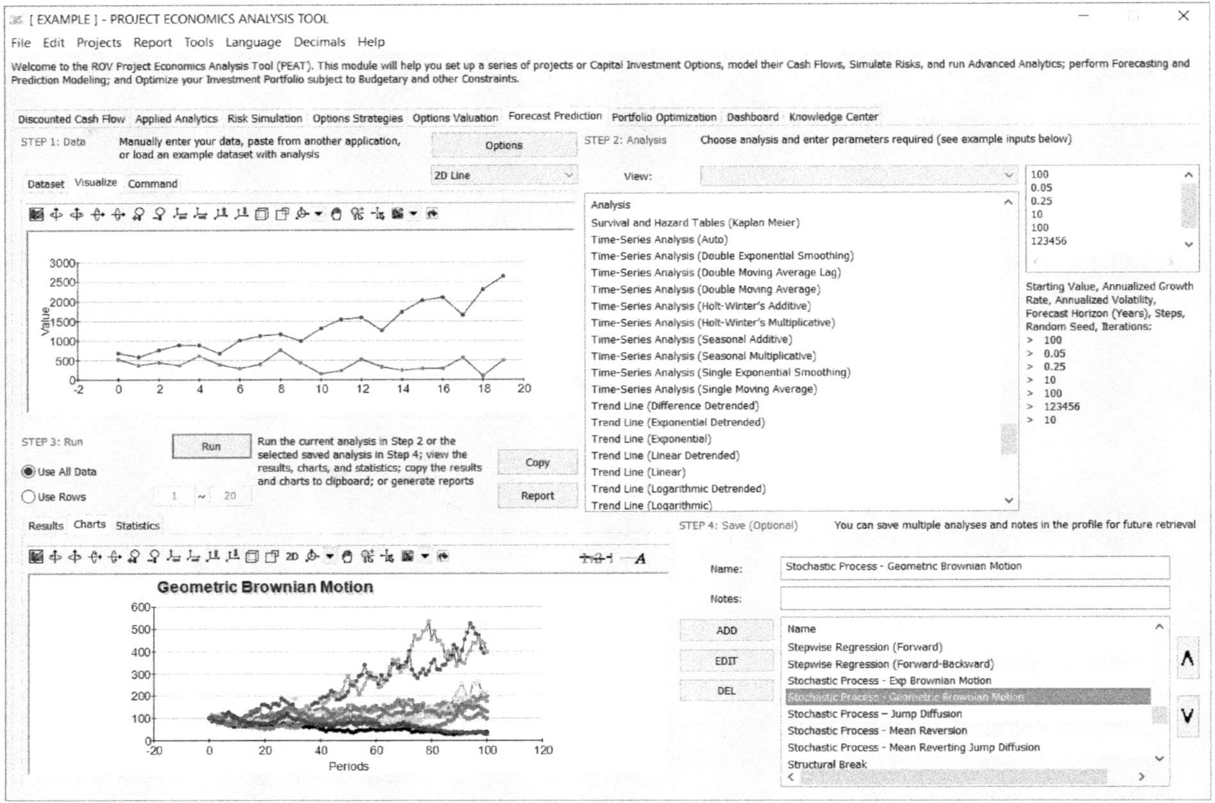

Figure 7.2 – Forecast Prediction: Data Visualization and Results Charts

File   Edit   Projects   Report   Tools   Language   Decimals   Help

Welcome to the ROV Project Economics Analysis Tool (PEAT). This module will help you set up a series of projects or Capital Investment Options, model their Cash Flows, Simulate Risks, and run Advanced Analytics; perform Forecasting and Prediction Modeling; and Optimize your Investment Portfolio subject to Budgetary and other Constraints.

Discounted Cash Flow   Applied Analytics   Risk Simulation   Options Strategies   Options Valuation   Forecast Prediction   Portfolio Optimization   Dashboard   Knowledge Center

STEP 1: Data   Manually enter your data, paste from another application, or load an example dataset with analysis

Dataset   Visualize   Command

2D Line

STEP 2: Analysis   Choose analysis and enter parameters required (see example inputs below)

View:

Analysis
Survival and Hazard Tables (Kaplan Meier)
Time-Series Analysis (Auto)
Time-Series Analysis (Double Exponential Smoothing)
Time-Series Analysis (Double Moving Average Lag)
Time-Series Analysis (Double Moving Average)
Time-Series Analysis (Holt-Winter's Additive)
Time-Series Analysis (Holt-Winter's Multiplicative)
Time-Series Analysis (Seasonal Additive)
Time-Series Analysis (Seasonal Multiplicative)
Time-Series Analysis (Single Exponential Smoothing)
Time-Series Analysis (Single Moving Average)
Trend Line (Difference Detrended)
Trend Line (Exponential Detrended)
Trend Line (Exponential)
Trend Line (Linear Detrended)
Trend Line (Linear)
Trend Line (Logarithmic Detrended)
Trend Line (Logarithmic)

Starting Value, Annualized Growth
Rate, Annualized Volatility,
Forecast Horizon (Years), Steps,
Random Seed, Iterations:
>   100
>   0.05
>   0.25
>   10
>   100
>   123456
>   10

100
0.05
0.25
10
100
123456

STEP 3: Run

Run   Run the current analysis in Step 2 or the selected saved analysis in Step 4; view the results, charts, and statistics; copy the results and charts to clipboard; or generate reports

○ Use All Data
○ Use Rows   1 ~ 20

Copy
Report

Results   Charts   Statistics

STEP 4: Save (Optional)   You can save multiple analyses and notes in the profile for future retrieval

Name: Stochastic Process - Geometric Brownian Motion

Notes:

ADD
EDIT
DEL

Name
Stepwise Regression (Forward)
Stepwise Regression (Forward-Backward)
Stochastic Process - Exp Brownian Motion
Stochastic Process - Geometric Brownian Motion
Stochastic Process – Jump Diffusion
Stochastic Process - Mean Reversion
Stochastic Process - Mean Reverting Jump Diffusion
Structural Break

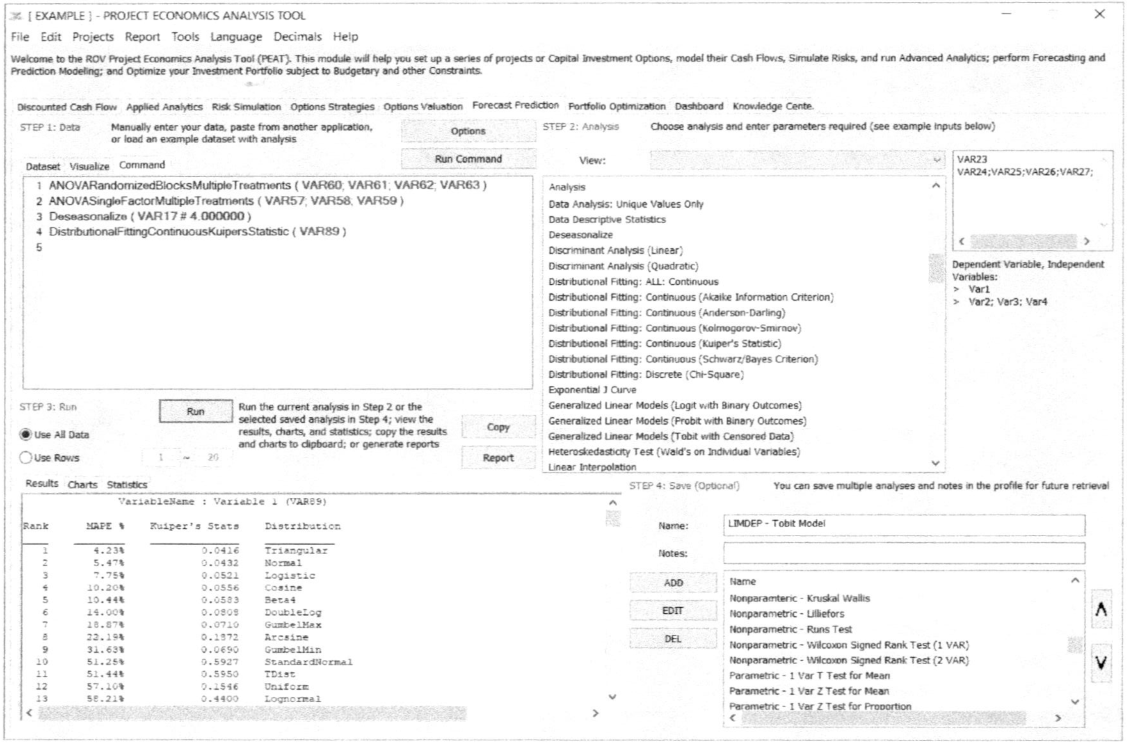

Figure 7.3 – Forecast Prediction: Command Console

PORTFOLIO OPTIMIZATION

In the *Portfolio Optimization* section, the individual Projects can be modeled as a portfolio and optimized to determine the best combination of projects for the portfolio. In today's competitive global economy, companies are faced with many difficult decisions. These decisions include allocating financial resources, building or expanding facilities, managing inventories, and determining product-mix strategies. Such decisions might involve thousands or millions of potential alternatives. Considering and evaluating each of them would be impractical or even impossible. A model can provide valuable assistance in incorporating relevant variables when analyzing decisions and in finding the best solutions for making decisions. Models capture the most important features of a problem and present them in a form that is easy to interpret. Models often provide insights that intuition alone cannot. An optimization model has three major elements: decision variables, constraints, and an objective. In short, the optimization methodology finds the best combination or permutation of decision variables (e.g., which products to sell and which projects to execute) in every conceivable way such that the objective is maximized (e.g., revenues and net income) or minimized (e.g., risk and costs) while still satisfying the constraints (e.g., budget and resources).

Important Note: The Optimization Settings cannot be set and optimizations cannot be run if you do not first run a Risk Simulation. Make sure you have first run a risk simulation model before attempting to set up an optimization model.

The Projects can be modeled as a portfolio and optimized to determine the best combination of projects for the portfolio in the *Optimization Settings* tab (Figure 8.1 shows the Optimization Settings of the DCF default example model after the *Simulate All Options at Once* selection was run in the Risk Simulation section). Select the decision variable type of *Discrete Binary* (chooses which Projects to execute with a Go/No-Go binary 1/0 decision) or *Continuous Budget Allocation* (returns % of budget to allocate to each Project as long as the total portfolio is 100%); select the *Objective* (e.g., Max NPV, Min Risk, etc.); set up any *Constraints* (e.g., budget or number of projects restrictions, or create your own customized restrictions); then select the Projects to optimize/allocate/choose (default selection is all Projects); and when completed, click *Run Optimization*. The software will then take you to the *Optimization Results* (Figure 8.1).

There are also some additional advanced capabilities in this settings tab. For instance, the *Compare Models* button allows you to select and run multiple saved optimization models to compare the results. This is useful if you wish to compare results side by side, multiple optimizations with different objectives. The *Custom Objective* and *Custom Constraints* allow you to create your own user-specified variables. *Enumeration* will run if there are less than a dozen decision variables and discrete go/no-go decisions are selected, where every possible combination and permutation will be tested, thereby taking a little longer to run than usual, but will guarantee a global optimum result. The *Advanced Settings* button allows you to set the precision of the solution, maximum number of iterations, runtime, phased optimization, as well as sequential starting decision variables when building the efficient frontier. Finally, you can use previously saved results to run the optimization or load and use the latest results based on the simulation you have just run, or manually override the inputs.

Decision Variables

Decision variables are quantities over which you have control, for example, the amount of a product to make, the number of dollars to allocate among different investments, or which projects to select from among a limited set. As an example, portfolio optimization analysis includes a go or no-go decision on particular projects. In addition, the dollar or percentage budget allocation across multiple projects also can be structured as decision variables.

Constraints

Constraints describe relationships among decision variables that restrict the values of the decision variables. For example, a constraint might ensure that the total amount of money allocated among various investments cannot exceed a specified amount or at most one project from a certain group can be selected; budget constraints; timing restrictions; minimum returns; or risk tolerance levels.

Objective

Objectives give a mathematical representation of the model's desired outcome, such as maximizing profit or minimizing cost, in terms of the decision variables. In financial analysis, for example, the objective may be to maximize returns while minimizing risks (maximizing the Sharpe's ratio or returns-to-risk ratio).

Portfolio Optimization | Optimization Results

The *Optimization Results* tab returns the results from the portfolio optimization analysis. For instance, Figure 8.2. shows the results after running the saved *Optimization Efficient Frontier – Budget* model from the *Optimization Settings* tab. The main results are provided in the data grid (lower left corner), showing the final Objective function result, final Constraints, and the allocation, selection, or optimization across all individual Projects within this optimized portfolio. The top left portion of the screen shows the textual details of the optimization algorithms applied, and the chart illustrates the final objective function (the chart will only show a single point for regular optimizations, whereas it will return an investment efficient frontier curve if the optional *Efficient Frontier* settings are set [min, max, step size] in the *Optimization Settings* tab).

File Edit Projects Report Tools Language Decimals Help

Welcome to the ROV Project Economics Analysis Tool (PEAT). This module will help you set up a series of projects or Capital Investment Options, model their Cash Flows, Simulate Risks, and run Advanced Analytics; perform Forecasting and Prediction Modeling; and Optimize your Investment Portfolio subject to Budgetary and other Constraints.

Discounted Cash Flow Applied Analytics Risk Simulation Options Strategies Options Valuation Forecast Prediction Portfolio Optimization Dashboard Knowledge Center

Optimization Settings Optimization Results Advanced Custom Optimization

Set the portfolio optimization parameters here. Be aware that to have a good set of portfolio optimization results, typically multiple Options need to be available and to have been modeled and simulated.

The optimization run has been completed.Optimize Time: 1s.

Saved Model

Optimization (Budgets and Projects)
Optimization (Efficient Frontier - Budget)
Optimization (Efficient Frontier - Projects)
Noneconomic Variables (Weighted Average of Customs)
Noneconomic Variables (Satisfy Demand)
Noneconomic Variables (Business Strategy)

Edit
Delete
Save
∧ ∨

Model Name: Optimization (Efficient Frontier - Budget)

Save As...
Clear

Step 1: Select the Decision Variable type:
● Discrete Binary Go or No-Go Decision
○ Continuous Budget Allocation Across the Portfolio

Step 2: Select an Objective:
Max Portfolio Return to Risk (Inverse CV)
Step 4: Select the Decision variables to optimize:

Custom Objective + -
☐ Manual Override

Step 3: Set your Constraints:

	Weight (%)	Relation	Value
✓ Number of Projects		= = ▸	
Total Investment		< = ▸	
Total Net Present Value		= = ▸	
Total Rate of Return		= = ▸	
☐ Custom Variable 1		= = ▸	
☐ Custom Variable 2		= = ▸	
☐ Custom Variable 3		= = ▸	
☐ Custom Variable 4		= = ▸	
☐ Custom Variable 5		= = ▸	
☐ Custom Variable 6		= = ▸	
☐ Custom Variable 7		= = ▸	
☐ Custom Variable 8		= = ▸	

Custom Constraints

Efficient Frontier (Optional)

Min	Max	Step Size
2000000	4000000	500000

● Use Previously Saved Results
○ Load and Use Latest Results

Run Optimization Advanced Settings
Compare Models... Enumeration

Decisions	Objective	Risk	Investment	Initial Decision	Custom 1	Custom 2	Custom 3	Custom 4	Custom 5	Custom 6	Custom 7	Custom 8	Weighted AVG
Portfolio Total:	7.81	12.81%	5,159,554.77	10									
▷ Option1	4.54	22.04%	250,000.00	1									
▷ Option2	3.57	28.01%	528,181.82	1									
▷ Option3	3.94	25.39%	55,000.00	1									
▷ Option4	3.50	28.59%	55,000.00	1									
▷ Option5	4.80	20.82%	83,000.00	1									
▷ Option6	4.90	20.41%	74,181.82	1									
▷ Option7	4.40	22.72%	2,440,909.09	1									
▷ Option8	4.69	21.32%	1,535,818.18	1									

Figure 8.1 – Portfolio Optimization: Optimization Settings

Welcome to the ROV Project Economics Analysis Tool (PEAT). This module will help you set up a series of projects or Capital Investment Options, model their Cash Flows, Simulate Risks, and run Advanced Analytics; perform Forecasting and Prediction Modeling; and Optimize your Investment Portfolio subject to Budgetary and other Constraints.

Discounted Cash Flow   Applied Analytics   Risk Simulation   Options Strategies   Options Valuation   Forecast Prediction   Portfolio Optimization   Dashboard   Knowledge Center

Optimization Settings   Optimization Results   Advanced Custom Optimization

Risk Optimizer Report: Date Sun Dec 30 16:08:40 2018 Runtime: 0.42 seconds

Problem Title: PEAT Portfolio Optimization

Problem Parameters:
Number of variables   10
Number of functions   2
Objective function will be MAXIMIZED

Starting Values

Functions:

No.	Function Name	Status	Type	Initial Value	Lower Bound	Upper Bound
1	G		RANGE	1.97682e+006	-1.79769e+306	2e+006
2	G		OBJ	6.12864		

Variables:

No.	Variable Name	Status		Initial Value	Lower Bound	Upper Bound

Chart Type: Standard 2D Line

☐ Show Values on Chart

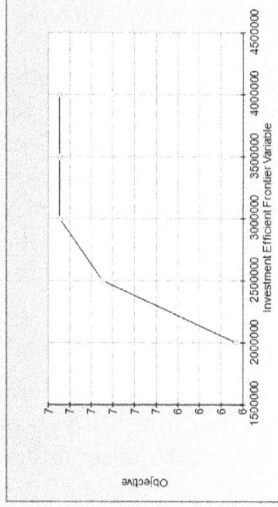

The optimization run has been completed.Optimize Time: 1s.

Objective Function	6.1286	6.7465	6.9478	6.9478	6.9478
Frontier Variable	2,000,000	2,500,000	3,000,000	3,500,000	4,000,000
Optimized Constraint	1,978,818	2,487,042	2,718,646	2,718,646	2,718,646
Option1	1	1	1	1	1
Option2	0	1	1	1	1
Option3	1	1	1	1	1
Option4	1	1	1	1	1
Option5	1	0	1	1	1
Option6	0	0	1	1	1
Option7	0	0	0	0	0
Option8	1	0	0	0	0
Option9	0	0	1	1	1
Option10	0	1	1	1	1

Figure 8.2 – Portfolio Optimization: Optimization Results

In the *Advanced Custom Optimization* tab (see Figures 8.3–8.7), you can create and solve your own optimization models. Knowledge of optimization modeling is required to set up your own models, but you can click on *Load Example* and select a sample model to run. You can use these sample models to learn how the Optimization routines can be set up. Click *Run* when done to execute the optimization routines and algorithms. The calculated results and charts will be presented on completion.

When setting up your own optimization model, we recommend going from one tab to another, starting with the Method (static, dynamic, or stochastic optimization); setting up the Decision Variables, Constraints, and Statistics (applicable only if simulation inputs have first been set up, and if dynamic or stochastic optimization is run); and setting the Objective function.

Method: Static Optimization

As far as the optimization process is concerned, PEAT's Advanced Custom Optimization can be used to run a Static Optimization, that is, an optimization that is run on a static model, where no simulations are run. In other words, all the inputs in the model are static and unchanging. This optimization type is applicable when the model is assumed to be known and no uncertainties exist. Also, a discrete optimization can be first run to determine the optimal portfolio and its corresponding optimal allocation of decision variables before more advanced optimization procedures are applied. For instance, before running a stochastic optimization problem, a discrete optimization is first run to determine if there exist solutions to the optimization problem before a more protracted analysis is performed.

Method: Dynamic Optimization

Next, Dynamic Optimization is applied when Monte Carlo simulation is used together with optimization. Another name for such a procedure is Simulation-Optimization. That is, a simulation is first run, then the results of the simulation are applied back into the model, and then an optimization is applied to the simulated values. In other words, a simulation is run for N trials, and then an optimization process is run for M iterations until the optimal results are obtained, or an infeasible set is found. That is, using PEAT's optimization module, you can choose which forecast and assumption statistics to use and replace in the model after the simulation is run. Then, these forecast statistics can be applied in the optimization process. This approach is useful when you have a large model with many interacting assumptions and forecasts, and when some of the forecast statistics are required in the optimization. For example, if the standard deviation of an assumption or forecast is required in the optimization model (e.g., computing the Sharpe ratio in asset allocation and optimization problems where we have mean divided by standard deviation of the portfolio), then this approach should be used.

Method: Stochastic Optimization

The Stochastic Optimization process, in contrast, is similar to the dynamic optimization procedure with the exception that the entire dynamic optimization process is repeated T times. That is, a simulation with N trials is run, and then an optimization is run with M iterations to obtain the optimal results. Then the process is replicated T times. The results will be a forecast chart of each decision variable with T values. In other words, a simulation is run and the forecast or assumption statistics are used in the optimization model to find the optimal allocation of decision variables. Then, another simulation is run, generating different forecast statistics, and these new updated values are then optimized, and so forth. Hence, the final decision variables will each have their own forecast chart, indicating the range of the optimal decision variables. For instance, instead of obtaining single-point estimates in the dynamic optimization procedure, you can now obtain a distribution of the decision variables and, hence, a range of optimal values for each decision variable, also known as a stochastic optimization.

TIPS on Optimization Method

- You should always run a *Static Optimization* prior to running any of the more advanced methods to test if the setup of your model is correct.

- The *Dynamic Optimization* and *Stochastic Optimization* must first have simulation assumptions set. That is, both of the approaches require Monte Carlo Risk Simulation to be run prior to starting the optimization routines.

Decision Variables

Decision variables are quantities over which you have control, for example, the amount of a product to make, the number of dollars to allocate among different investments, or which projects to select from among a limited set. As an example, portfolio optimization analysis includes a go or no-go decision on particular projects. In addition, the dollar or percentage budget allocation across multiple projects also can be structured as decision variables.

TIPS on Optimization Decision Variables

- Click *Add* to add a new *Decision Variable*. You can also *Change*, *Delete*, or *Duplicate* an existing decision variable.

- *Decision Variables* can be set as *Continuous* (with lower and upper bounds), *Integers* (with lower and upper bounds), *Binary* (0 or 1), or a *Discrete Range*.

- The list of available variables is shown in the data grid, complete with their assumptions.

Constraints

Constraints describe relationships among decision variables that restrict the values of the decision variables. For example, a constraint might ensure that the total amount of money allocated among various investments cannot exceed a specified amount or, at most, one project from a certain group can be selected; budget, timing, minimum returns, or risk tolerance levels are other examples of constraints.

TIPS on Optimization Constraints

- Click *Add* to add a new *Constraint*. You can also *Change* or *Delete* an existing constraint.

- When you add a new constraint, the list of available *Variables* will be shown. Simply double-click on a desired variable and its variable syntax will be added to the *Expression* window. For example, double-clicking on a variable named "Return1" will create a syntax variable "$(Return1)$" in the window.

- Enter your own constraint equation. For example, the following is a constraint:

  $(Asset1)$+$(Asset2)$+$(Asset3)$+$(Asset4)$=1, where the sum of all four decision variables must add up to 1.

- Keep adding as many constraints as you need but be aware that the higher the number of constraints, the longer the optimization will take, and the higher the probability of your making an error or creating nonbinding constraints or having constraints that violate another existing constraint (thereby introducing an error in your model).

Statistics

The Statistics subtab will be populated only if there are simulation assumptions set up.

TIPS on Optimization Statistics

- The *Statistics* window will only be populated if you have previously defined simulation assumptions available.

- If there are simulation assumptions set up, you can run *Dynamic Optimization* or *Stochastic Optimization;* otherwise you are restricted to running only *Static Optimizations*.

- In the window, you can click on the statistics individually to obtain a drop-down list. Here you can select the statistic to apply in the optimization process. The default is to return the *Mean* from the Monte Carlo Risk Simulation and replace the variable with the chosen statistic (in this case the average value), and Optimization will then be executed based on this statistic.

Objective

Objectives give a mathematical representation of the model's desired outcome, such as maximizing profit or minimizing cost, in terms of the decision variables. In financial analysis, for example, the objective may be to maximize returns while minimizing risks (maximizing the Sharpe's ratio or returns-to-risk ratio).

TIPS on Optimization Objective

- You can enter your own customized *Objective* in the function window. The list of available variables is shown in the *Variables* window on the right. This list includes predefined decision variables and simulation assumptions.

- An example of an objective function equation looks something like:

($(Asset1)$*$(AS_Return1)$+$(Asset2)$*$(AS_Return2)$+$(Asset3)$*$(AS_Return3)$+$(Asset4)$*$(AS_Return4)$)/sqrt((AS_Risk1)**2*$(Asset1)$**2+(AS_Risk2)**2*$(Asset2)$**2+(AS_Risk3)**2*$(Asset3)$**2+(AS_Risk4)**2*$(Asset4)$**2)

- You can use some of the most common math operators such as +, -, *, /, **, where the latter is the function for "raised to the power of."

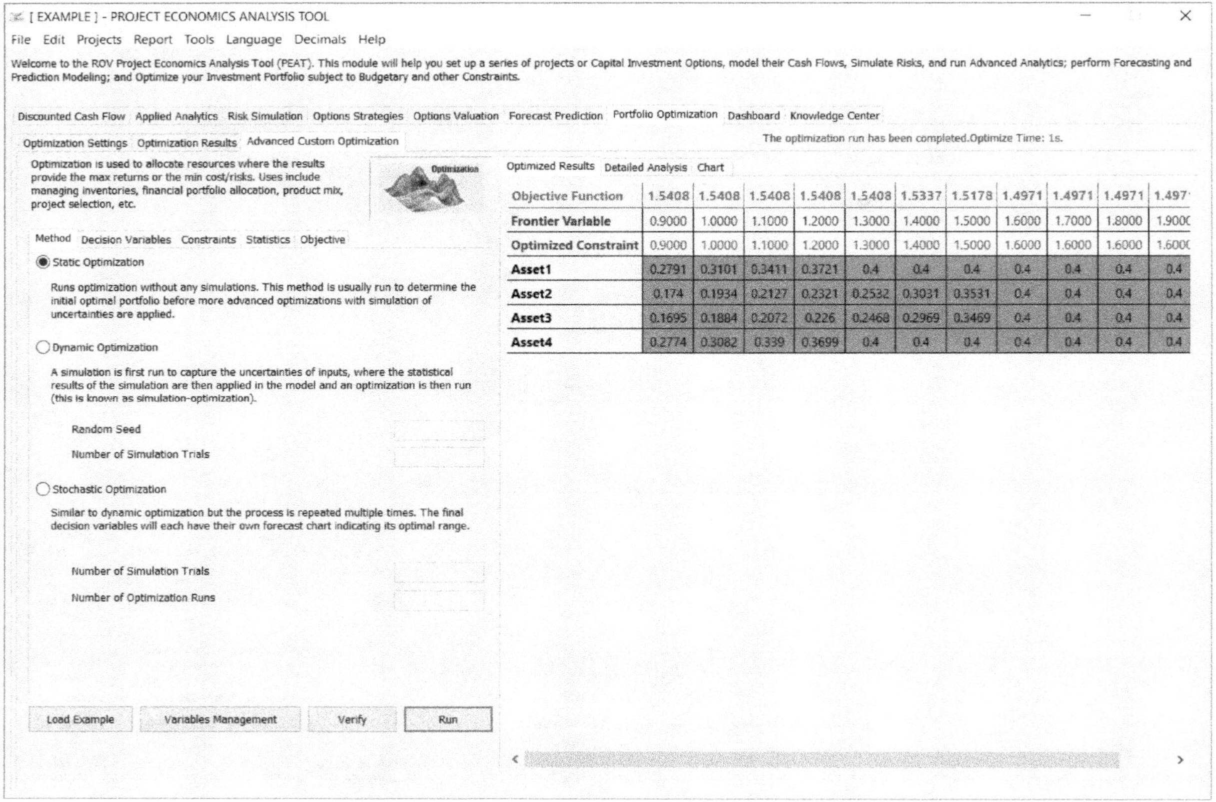

Figure 8.3 – Portfolio Optimization: Method

File Edit Projects Report Tools Language Decimals Help

Welcome to the ROV Project Economics Analysis Tool (PEAT). This module will help you set up a series of projects or Capital Investment Options, model their Cash Flows, Simulate Risks, and run Advanced Analytics; perform Forecasting and Prediction Modeling; and Optimize your Investment Portfolio subject to Budgetary and other Constraints.

Discounted Cash Flow Applied Analytics Risk Simulation Options Strategies Options Valuation Forecast Prediction Portfolio Optimization Dashboard Knowledge Center

Optimization Settings Optimization Results Advanced Custom Optimization

Optimization is used to allocate resources where the results provide the max returns or the min cost/risks. Users include managing inventories, financial portfolio allocation, product mix, project selection, etc.

The optimization run has been completed.Optimize Time: 1s.

Method Decision Variables Constraints Statistics Objective

Name	Type	Rules	Starting Value
Asset1	Continuous	0.100000 to 0.400000	0.250000
Asset2	Continuous	0.100000 to 0.400000	0.250000
Asset3	Continuous	0.100000 to 0.400000	0.250000
Asset4	Continuous	0.100000 to 0.400000	0.250000

Add Change Delete Duplicate

Load Example Variables Management Verify Run

Optimized Results Detailed Analysis Chart

Risk Optimizer Report: Date Sun Dec 30 16:11:11s 2018 Runtime: 0.14 seconds

Problem Title: Optimization - Efficient Frontier

Problem Parameters:
Number of Variables 4
Number of Functions 2
Objective Function will be Maximized

Starting Values

Functions:

No.	Function Name	Status	Type	Initial Value	Lower Bound	Upper Bound
1	G	****	RNGE	1		
2	G		OBJ	1.4970s	0.9	0.9

Variables:

No.	Variable Name	Status	Initial Value	Lower Bound	Upper Bound
1	Asset1		0.25	0.1	0.4
2	Asset2		0.25	0.1	0.4
3	Asset3		0.25	0.1	0.4
4	Asset4		0.25	0.1	0.4

Final Results

Functions:

Itn No.	Objective Function	Binding Constrs	Super Basics	Infeas Constr	Norm of Red.Grad	Hessian Cond.No.	Step Size	Degen Step
0	0.1	4	0	4	1.0	1	0.025	
1	1.4974	4	3	0	0.54	10	0.095	
3	1.5408	3	3	0	0.019	5.4	0.083	
4	1.5408	3	3	0	0.016	2.1	0.0012	
5	1.5408	1	1	0	7e-006	2.1	0.0017	

No.	Name	Status	Initial Value	Final Value	Status	Distance from Nearest Bound	Lagrange Multiplier
1	G		1	0.9	Upperbnd	2e-010	
2	G		1.4971	1.5408	Objective		:u -2.9754e-006

Variables:

EXAMPLE 1 - PROJECT ECONOMICS ANALYSIS TOOL

File Edit Projects Report Tools Language Decimals Help

Welcome to the ROV Project Economics Analysis Tool (PEAT). This module will help you set up a series of projects or Capital Investment Options, model their Cash Flows, Simulate Risks, and run Advanced Analytics; perform Forecasting and Prediction Modeling; and Optimize your Investment Portfolio subject to Budgetary and other Constraints.

Discounted Cash Flow Applied Analytics Risk Simulation Options Strategies Options Valuation Forecast Prediction Portfolio Optimization Dashboard Knowledge Center

Optimization Settings Optimization Results Advanced Custom Optimization

Optimization is used to allocate resources where the results provide the max returns or the min cost/risks. Uses include managing inventories, financial portfolio allocation, product mix, project selection, etc.

The optimization run has been completed.Optimize Time: 1s.

Optimized Results Detailed Analysis Chart

Chart Type: Standard 2D Line

☐ Show Values on Chart

Method Decision Variables Constraints Statistics Objective

Expression

☑ $(Asset1)$+$(Asset2)$+$(Asset3)$+$(Asset4)$=$...

Add

Change

Selected Item

$(Asset1)$+$(Asset2)$+$(Asset

Load Example   Variab

1.545

1.54

1.535

Constraints Properties   ×

Expression

$(Asset1)$+$(Asset2)$+$(Asset3)$+$(Asset4)$=$(Limit)$

Variables   Frontier Variables

Name   Name

Asset1   Limit

Asset2
Asset3
Asset4

Add

Edit

Delete

Double Click a Variable or
Frontier Variable to bring it into
the above expression

OK

Cancel

1.4 1.6 1.8 2 2.2
Fro Var

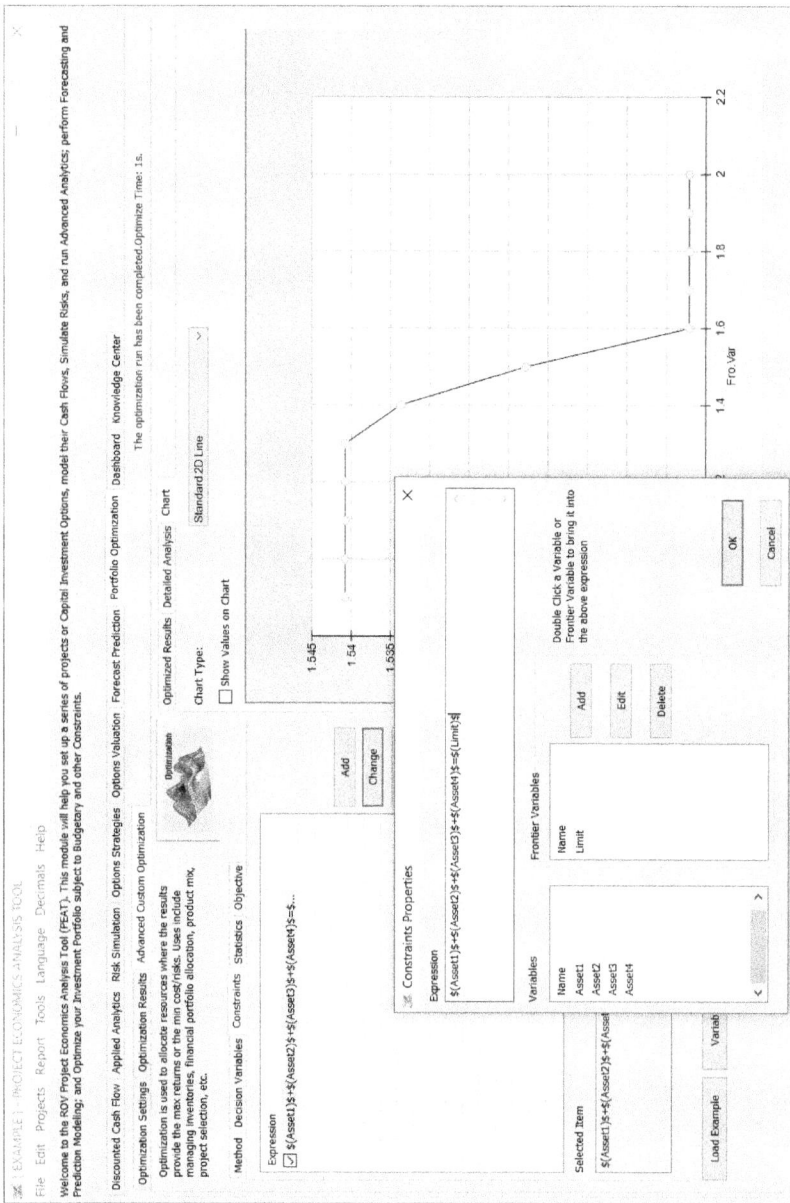

Figure 8.5 – Portfolio Optimization: Constraints

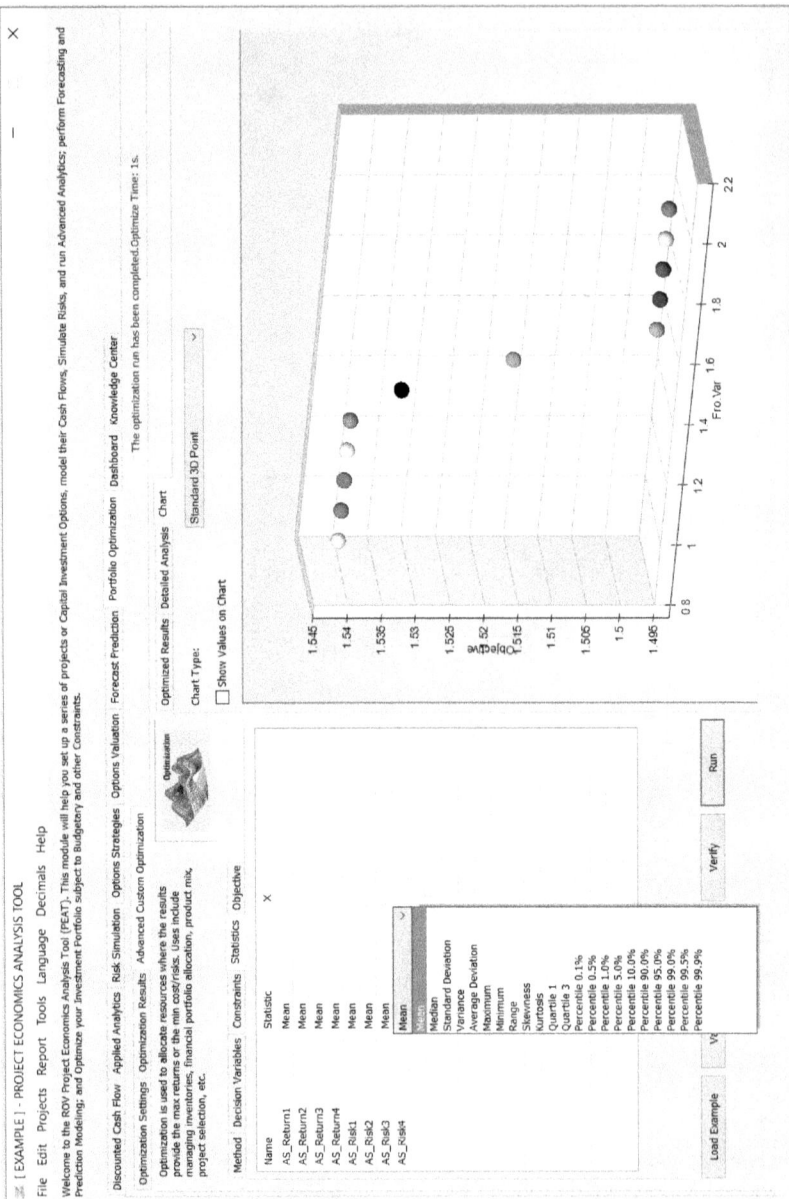

Figure 8.6 – Portfolio Optimization: Statistics

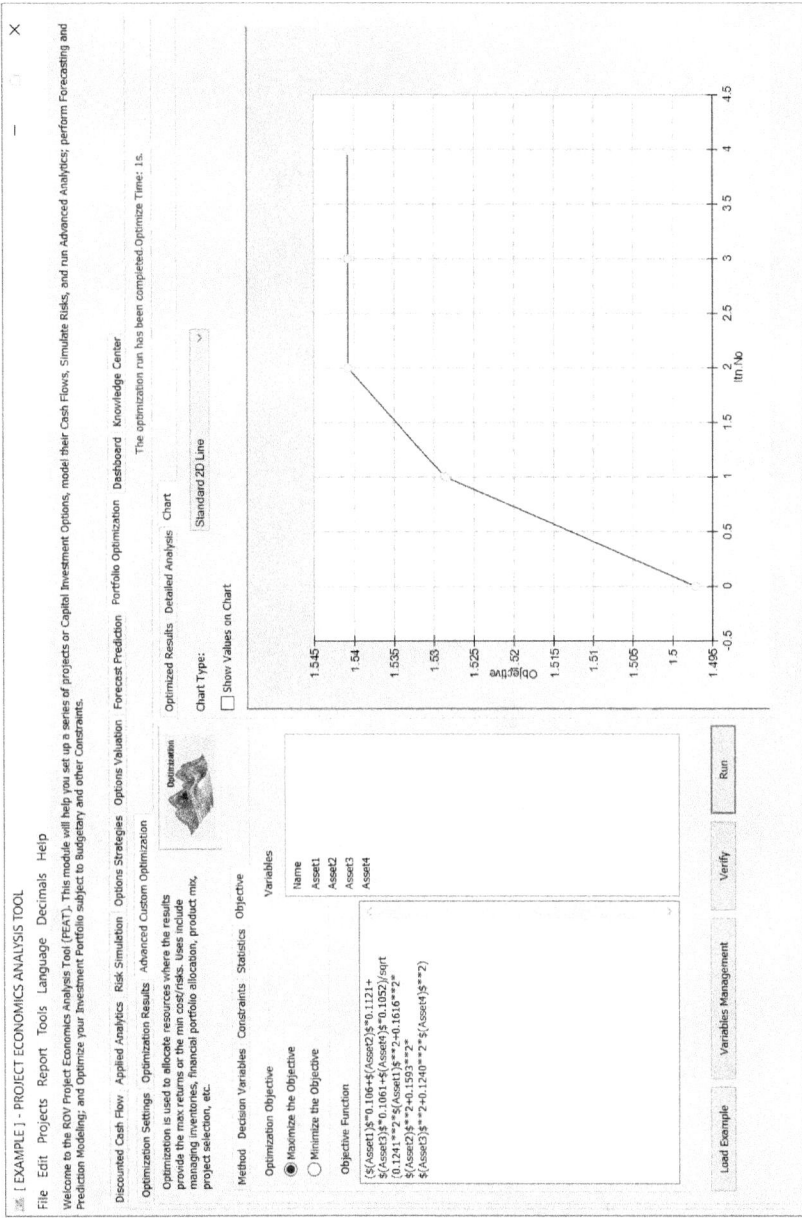

Figure 8.7 – Portfolio Optimization: Objective

DASHBOARD, KNOWLEDGE MANAGEMENT, AND OPTIONS

Discount Rates

In the Discounted Cash Flow module, we have a *Discount Rates* tab. This tab allows the user to compute an appropriate discount rate to use in the project valuation. For instance, the two subtabs are:

- *Weighted Average Cost of Capital (WACC).* This is an optional set of analytics whereby you can compute the firm's WACC to use as a discount rate (Figure 9.1). Start by selecting either the *Simple WACC* or *Detailed WACC Cost Elements.* Then, you can either enter the required inputs or click on the *Load Example* button to load a sample set of inputs that you can use as a guide for entering your own set of assumptions.

- *Beta.* This is another optional subtab used for computing the Beta risk coefficient by pasting in historical stock prices or stock returns to compute the Beta (Figure 9.2). The resulting Beta is used in the Capital Asset Pricing Model (CAPM), one of the main inputs into the WACC model. Start by selecting whether you have historical *Stock Prices* or *Stock Returns*, then enter the number of *Rows* (periods) of historical data you have and *Paste* the data into the relevant columns and click *Compute.* The Beta result will update, and you can use this Beta as an input into the WACC model.

In the Discounted Cash Flow module, the *WACC* and *BETA* calculations are available under the *Discount Rate* subtab of the main *DCF* tab.

When deciding on the periodicity and length of historical stock price data to use, we recommend using daily stock prices with an historical period either commensurate with the Project's analysis period or a representative period in the past (similar risks and market conditions in the past that are expected to repeat themselves in the near future).

Custom Calculations

A *Custom* tab (Figure 9.3) is also available for making your own custom calculations just as you would in an Excel spreadsheet. Clicking on the *Function F(x)* button will provide you with a list of the supported functions you can use in this tab. Other basic mathematical functions are also supported, such as =, +, -, /, *, ^. If you use this optional *Custom Calculations* tab and wish to link some cells to the input tabs (e.g., Project 1), you can select the cells in the *Custom Calculations* tab, right-click, and select *Link To*. Then proceed to the location in the *Project* tabs and highlight the location of the input cells you wish to link to, right-click, and select *Link From*. Any subsequent changes you make in the *Custom Calculations* tab will be updated in the linked input assumption cells.

Example 1: In the *Custom Calculations* tab, enter the following: *1, 2, 3* into cells *A1, B1, C1,* respectively. Then in cell *D1,* enter =*A1+B1+C1* and click on any other cell and it will update the cell and return the value 6. Similarly, you type in =*SUM(A1:C1)* to obtain the same results. The preset functions can be seen by clicking on the *f(x)* the button.

Example 2: In the *Custom Calculations* tab, enter the following: *1, 2, 3* into cells *A1, B1, C1,* respectively. Then, *select these three cells, right-click,* and select *Link To*. Proceed to any one of the *Project* tabs, and in the *Discounted Cash Flow* or *Input Assumptions* subtabs, *select three cells across* (e.g., on the Revenue line item), *right-click* and select *Link From*. The values of cells *A1, B1, C1* in the *Custom Calculations* tab will be linked to this location. You can go back to the *Custom Calculations* tab and change the values in the original three cells and you will see the linked cells in the *Discounted Cash Flow* or *Input Assumptions* subtabs change and update to reflect the new values.

TIPS on the Custom Tab

- The *Custom* tab is where you can replicate your Excel models with multiple worksheets or multiple Excel workbooks so that all the preliminary calculations linked to your project will be stored in one convenient place, ready for auditing and archiving the models.

- In PEAT, click on *Help | Extras | PEAT Visual Guide 08 – Custom Tab and Excel Links* for a visual guide of these *Custom* tab's tips.

- Click on the *Custom* tab and then right-mouse-click to *Add* additional tabs, *Delete* existing tabs, *Duplicate*, *Rename*, and *Rearrange* Custom tabs.

- You can manually move and resize the column widths or click the *Grid...* button to select *Auto Fit* or set a specific width size.

- You can click on the *FX* icon to bring up a list of currently supported functions (e.g., ABS, AVERAGE, CONCATENATE, LEFT, LEN, LN, LOG, LOG10, MAX, MIN, POWER, RIGHT, ROUND, SUM, SUMIF, SUMPRODUCT, IF, AND, OR, +, -, /, *, ^).

- You can Name Cells (select one or more cells, type in the name you want in the cell Name box on the top left of the data grid and hit Enter). These named cells will appear later in Tornado, Scenario, and Risk Simulation tabs for easier recognition. If more than one cell is selected, then the cells will have the same name followed by an index (e.g., MyName1, MyName2, MyName3, etc.).

- Note that you can have multiple *Custom* tabs and rename them as you wish; each tab also has an internal name such as *xls1*, *xls2*, and so forth. These internal names are used in the software's internal algorithms as well as when you cross-link cells (linking across different *Custom* tabs, see below).

- You can copy existing calculations and worksheets from Excel and paste them into the *Custom* tabs. Simply select the cells or area in the Excel model worksheet you wish to copy, then *CTRL+C* or *right-mouse-click Copy* or click on the *Copy icon* in Excel. Then, select a cell in the Custom worksheet and hit *CTRL+V* or *right-mouse-click Paste* to paste into the Custom worksheet. Note that this approach will only paste the Texts and Values. Colors, equations, functions, live calculations, and formatting will not be included.

- Alternatively, you can paste a *Live Excel Model* with computations into the Custom worksheet:

  o In your Excel model, click *CTRL~* (hold down the *Control* key while hitting the *tilde* ~ key, which is usually located to the top left of the number 1 and letter Q keys) to change the Excel view from values and results to Equation View where you can see all the equations and functions. Once you are in the Equation View, you can copy from Excel and paste into PEAT's Custom worksheet as usual, and the equations will carry forward into the *Custom* tab. Equations will be pasted into the Custom worksheet and be updated/calculated as live links.

  o Please note that PEAT Custom worksheet now supports the main basic functions, which are sufficient for most users.

  o Uncheck the *Auto Calculate* box to temporarily turn off auto update before pasting a large model but remember to turn it back on afterwards. The *Custom* tab will paste the model more quickly.

  o Be careful with the specific cell locations where you copy and paste. For example, if you copy cells A1:C10 in Excel, make sure to paste into the same cell locations in the *Custom* tab so that the equations, links, and their computations will be preserved.

  o You can *Cross Link* cells among tabs (i.e., one custom tab has cells linked to another custom tab inside PEAT). In order to cross-link among tabs, you have to use the internal *Custom* tab naming convention. For example, you can use equations like: =xls2!a3 or =100*xls3!c35 and so forth. This is similar to Excel's worksheet cross-linking convention.

○ If you are copy and pasting a live model with multiple worksheet cross-linking via the CTRL~ approach above, make sure to *first rename your Excel worksheets to xls1, xls2, and so forth.* This will automatically rename the links inside Excel, and, hence, when you paste the live equations, the Custom tab cross-links will be maintained.

○ Another approach is to *Link to an External Excel Model.* This means the Excel model is kept separate and external from PEAT and will be maintained external to PEAT. These external Excel files can then be linked to PEAT and when the Excel source models are updated, the *Custom* tab's values will also be updated. In the Custom worksheet, click the *Excel* button to *Add an Excel Link* (or to Edit/Delete existing links). Then *Browse the Excel File* you need, select the *Excel Worksheet* and *Excel Cell Range* to link from, and enter the *Starting Cell* in the Custom worksheet to link to. Enter a *Name* and *Notes* for easy reference in the event you have multiple links (you can link multiple Excel workbook files and Excel worksheets) into one or more Custom worksheet. Be careful with the specific cell locations where you copy and paste. For example, if you copy cells A1:C10 in Excel, make sure to paste into the same cell locations in the *Custom* tab so that the equations, links, and their computations will be preserved.

• *Custom* tab's results and values can also be used to *Link From/To* another *Project* tab within the PEAT software. For instance, the *Custom* tab is used as a scratch location where your own custom computations are done. And some of these resulting computations need to be used in the *Project* tabs. You can always copy and paste static values to these *Project* tabs or create a dynamic updatable link. Multiple links can be performed, where each link can take on multiple cells at once.

○ The first step is a Link To. In the Custom worksheet, select the data area (one or more contiguous cells) and *right-mouse-click Link To* in order to generate a link from this Custom worksheet. Notice the blinking marquee border around a live Linked To data area.

- The second step is a *Link From*. In the *Project* tab, select the cells/location you wish to link the data into and right-mouse-click then select *Link From*. You can also *Remove Link* later if required. Notice the yellow highlights indicating a live link. Changing the values in the Custom worksheet will change the values here.

- Miscellaneous Tips

  - You right-mouse-click to *Copy Formula* and then right-mouse-click **Paste the Formula with Relative versus Absolute** cell addressing. This is the same as $ cell addressing in Excel. You can also paste data with Signs Reversed (e.g., expenses with -100 values will be pasted as 100 with signs reversed) or paste their Absolute Values regardless of signs.

  - You can also select cells with basic input values via the right-mouse-click and *Set as Simulation Assumptions*. These cells will turn green and show up later in the *Risk Simulation | Set Input Assumptions* tab. In the event these set assumption cells in the *Custom* tabs do not show up, save the file and reopen to reestablish their internal links.

  - Change cell *colors* or font colors by using the color droplist icons.

  - Use the *Up/Down/Left/Right* arrows on the keyboard to navigate the data grid.

  - Use *F2* or *double-click* on a cell to access the contents of the cell for editing.

  - Click on the *top left corner* of the data grid to select all cells at once.

  - You can increase/decrease the column width as required (simply drag the column to change its width or use the *Grid…* button to Auto-fit columns).

  - You can click on and select multiple rows or columns at once.

o   Do not change the source Excel file name or folder location if you are performing a live link from Excel.

o   By default, the Live Links from source Excel files are updated every time the *.rovprojecon file opens (this checkbox is default selected when you click on the Excel button in the Custom worksheet).

o   Live Excel links when updating and will locate the same file name in the absolute folder path (e.g., c:\your folder\subfolder name\filename.xlsx) first. If the file does not exist, it will locate the same file name in the relative folder path where your *.rovprojecon file is stored. The latter comes in handy when you have to e-mail the model file as well as the Excel source file to another individual, who may save the files in a different subdirectory/location/path but as long as both files reside in the same subfolder, the links will still update and work.

o   The best way to update any externally linked Excel files is to SAVE and restart the *rovprojecon file.

o   Manually inputted cells (black font) can be overridden easily by simply typing over the cell's values (type over the cell, double-click, or F2 to access and edit the cell). Linked cells (blue font) are intentionally created to prevent accidental overrides (you cannot simply type over existing cell values) and you can only intentionally override Excel linked cells by selecting the cell and editing its contents in the Formula bar.

File   Edit   Projects   Report   Tools   Language   Decimals   Help

Welcome to the ROV Project Economics Analysis Tool (PEAT). This module will help you set up a series of projects or Capital Investment Options, model their Cash Flows, Simulate Risks, and run Advanced Analytics; perform Forecasting and Prediction Modeling; and Optimize your Investment Portfolio subject to Budgetary and other Constraints.

Custom (xls1)   Project 1   Project 2   Project 3   Project 4   Project 5   Project 6   Project 7   Project 8   Project 9   Project 10   Portfolio Analysis   Discount Rates

Discounted Cash Flow   Applied Analytics   Risk Simulation   Options Strategies   Options Valuation   Forecast Prediction   Portfolio Optimization   Dashboard   Knowledge Center

WACC Beta

○ Use Simple WACC   Load Example

● Model Detailed WACC Cost Elements $ (Dollar)   ▼

1. COST OF DEBT, r_d (1 - T)

Years to Maturity (.)	30.00
Number of Payments Per Year (.)	2.00
Annual Coupon Rate (%)	9.000%
Bond Par Value ($)	$1,000.00
Current Bond Price ($)	$904.91
Corporate Marginal Tax Rate (%)	40.00%
Debt Flotation Cost (%)	0.000%
Annualized Cost of Debt (r_d)	10.005%
After Tax Cost of Debt (r_d)	6.003%

2. COST OF PREFERRED STOCK, r_{ps}

Preferred Stock's Dividend ($)	$8.00
Par Value ($)	$100.00
Stock Flotation Cost (%)	2.500%
Net Preferred Stock Issue Price (P_{net})	$97.50
Cost of Preferred Stock r_{ps} (%)	8.205%

3. COST OF COMMON STOCK, r_s

3A. THE CAPM APPROACH

Risk-Free Rate r_f (%)	5.000%
Market Return r_m (%)	10.500%
Stock Beta (.)	1.20
Cost of Common Stock (r_s)	11.600%

3B. THE DISCOUNTED CASH FLOW APPROACH

● Use Constant Growth Rate

○ Use Payout Ratio and Return on Equity

Stock Price P_0 ($)	$32.00
Dividend Payment D_1 ($)	$1.82
Constant Growth Rate g (%)	5.365%
Payout Rate (%)	63.000%
Return on Equity (%)	14.500%
Stock Floatation Cost F (%)	5.000%
Cost of Common Stock r_s	11.352%

3C. THE BOND-YIELD PLUS JUDGMENTAL-RISK PREMIUM APPROACH

Judgmental Over-Bond-Yield Risk Premium (%)	3.000%
Equivalent Corporate Bond Annualized Yield (%)	9.000%
Cost of Common Stock r_s	12.000%

3D. COMPARISON OF CAPM, DCF, BOND-YIELD PREMIUM

CAPM (r_s)	11.600%
Constant Growth DCF (r_s)	11.352%
Bond Yield Plus Risk-Premium (r_s)	12.000%
Average Cost of Common Stock (r_s)	11.651%

4. WEIGHTED AVERAGE COST OF CAPITAL (WACC)

Corporate Marginal Tax Rate (%)	40.000%
Weight of Debt (%)	30.000%
Weight of Preferred Stock (%)	10.000%
Weight of Common Stock (%)	60.000%
Weighted Average Cost of Capital WACC (%)	9.612%

Figure 9.1 – WACC Discount Rate

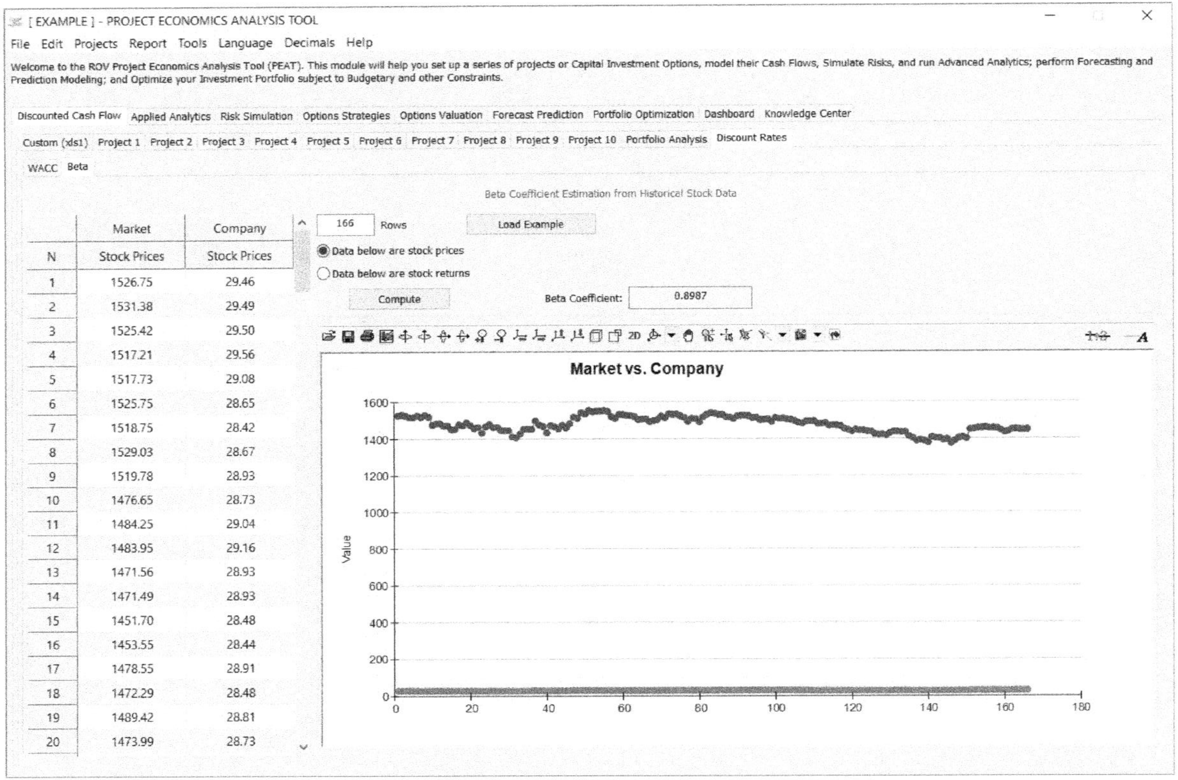

Figure 9.2 – Beta Risk Coefficient

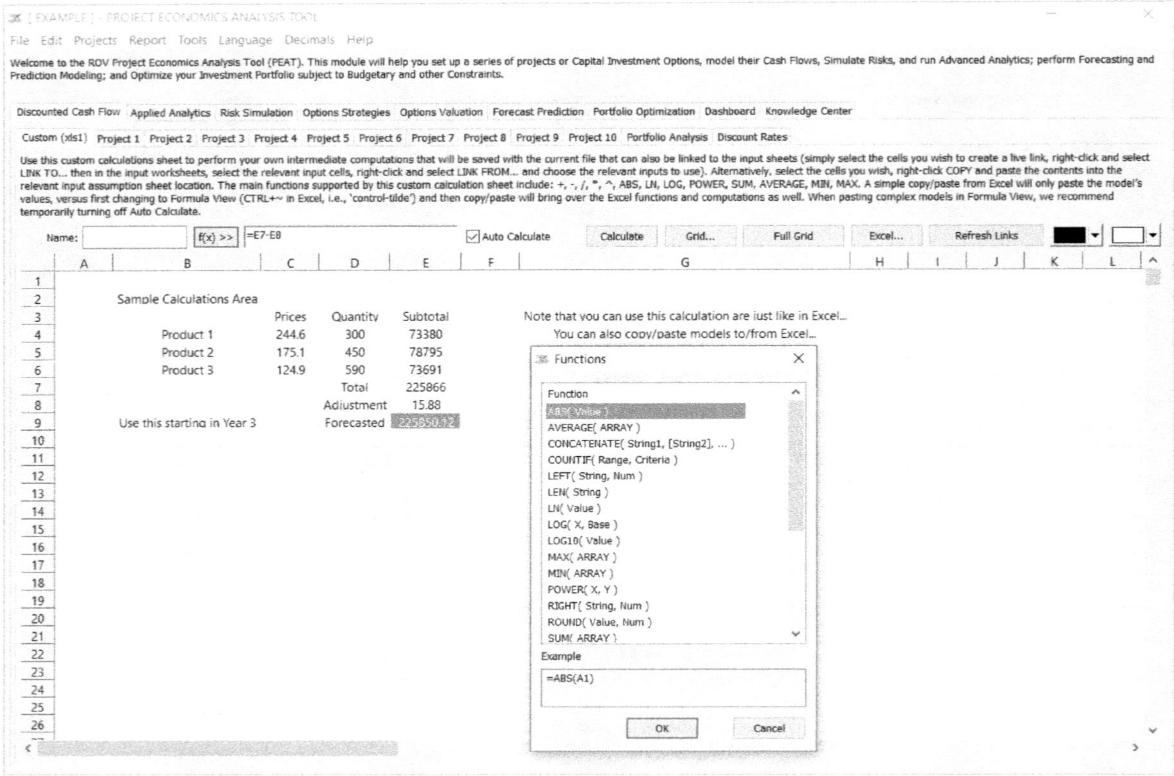

Figure 9.3 – Custom Calculations

This section on *Management Dashboards* (see Figures 9.4 and 9.5) shows how the results from the PEAT software can be summarized into management dashboards. To follow along, we assume that you are continuing to use the default DCF example and have already run risk simulation and optimization models. Then, click on the *Dashboard* tab (Figure 9.4) and wait for a few second while the software identifies and looks up the results in memory.

Then for each of the four available quadrants, select from the droplists what you would like to show (charts, data grids, text results, or your custom text). Remember to *Save* the dashboards when you are done setting them up. Then click on *View Dashboards* to view them (Figures 9.5 and 9.6). When viewing the dashboards, remember to click on the droplist to select which saved dashboard you wish to view. You can also click on *Capture Screen* to copy the quadrants and subsequently paste them into another software, like Microsoft PowerPoint and Excel.

In future versions of PEAT, the dashboards will have additional available configurations and settings, as well as allow for saving and archiving of dashboard results.

Knowledge Center | Step-by-Step Procedures

In the *Knowledge Center* (see Figures 9.7, 9.8, and 9.9), you will find quick getting started guides and sample procedures that are straight to the point to assist you in quickly getting up to speed in using the software. Click on the *Previous* and *Next* buttons to navigate from slide to slide or to view the *Getting Started Videos*. While these sessions are meant to provide a quick overview to help you get started with using PEAT, they do not substitute for years of experience or the technical knowledge required in the Certified in Quantitative Risk Management (CQRM) programs.

The Step-by-Step Procedures (Figure 9.7) highlights some quick getting started steps in a self-paced learning environment that is incorporated within the PEAT software. Navigate to this subtab within the Knowledge Center and click on the *Previous* and *Next* buttons to navigate from slide to slide. There are short descriptions above each slide, and key elements of the slide are highlighted in yellow for quick identification.

Knowledge Center | Basic Project Economics Lessons

The *Basic Project Economic Lessons* (Figure 9.8) provide an overview tour of some common concepts involved with cash flow analysis and project economic analysis such as the computations of NPV, IRR, MIRR, PI, ROI, PP, DPP, and so forth.

Knowledge Center | Getting Started Videos

Click on any one of the *Getting Started Videos* (Figure 9.9) to watch a short description and hands-on examples of how to run one of the sections within this PEAT software. The first quick getting started video is preinstalled with the software while the rest of the videos will have to be downloaded at first viewing. Make sure you have a good Internet connection to view these online videos.

TIPS on Knowledge Center

- The *Knowledge Center* files (videos, slides, and figures) are available in the installation path's three subfolders: *Lessons*, *Videos*, and *Procedures*. You can access the raw files directly or modify/update these files, and the updated files will show in the software tool's *Knowledge Center* the next time you re-start the software.

- Use the existing files (e.g., file type such as *.BMP or *.WMV as well as pixel size of figures) as a guide to the relevant file specifications you can use when replacing any of these original *Knowledge Center* files.

- If you wish to edit the text shown in the *Knowledge Center*, you can edit the *.*XML* files in the three subfolders, and the next time the software is started, the updated text will be shown.

- The *.*WMV* (Windows Media Video) file format is preferred as all Windows-based computers can run the video without any additional need for Video Codec installations. This file format is small in size and, hence, more portable when implementing it in the PEAT software tool installation build, such that you can still e-mail the installation build without the need for uploading to an FTP site. There are no minimum or maximum size limitations to this file format.

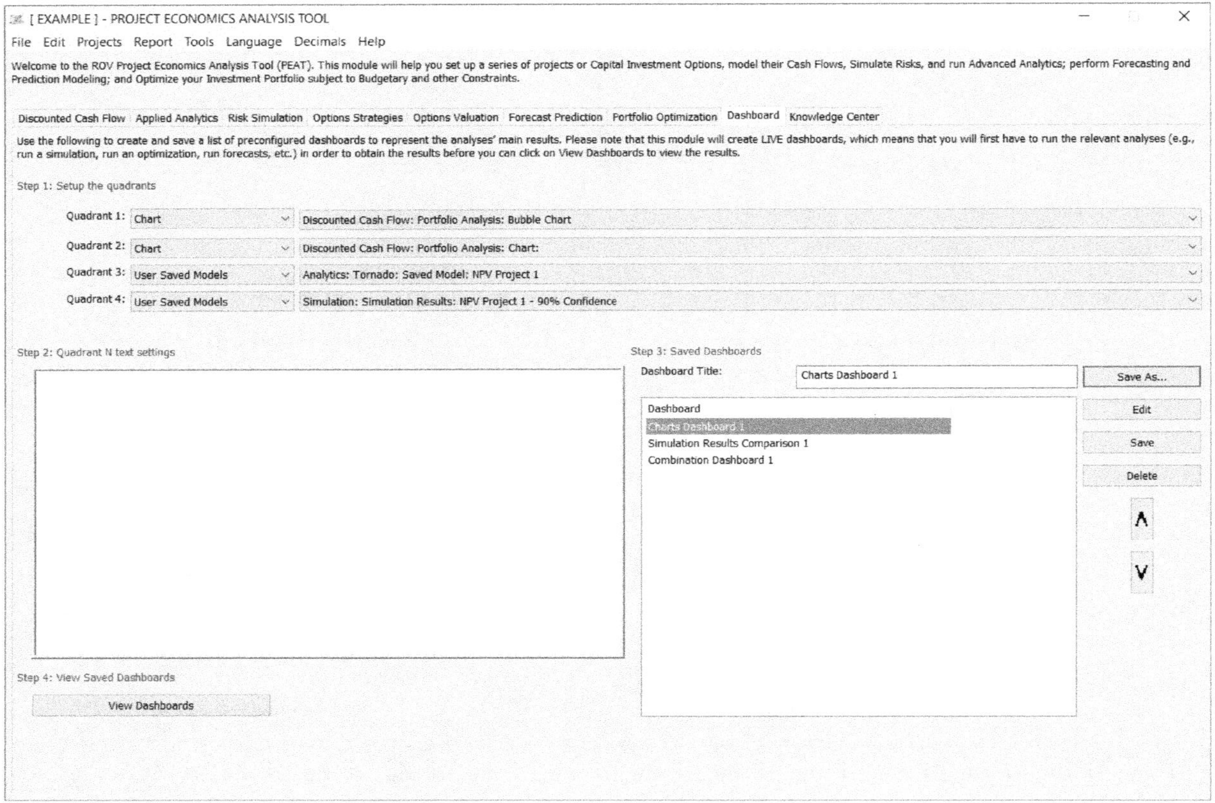

Figure 9.4 – Dashboard Settings

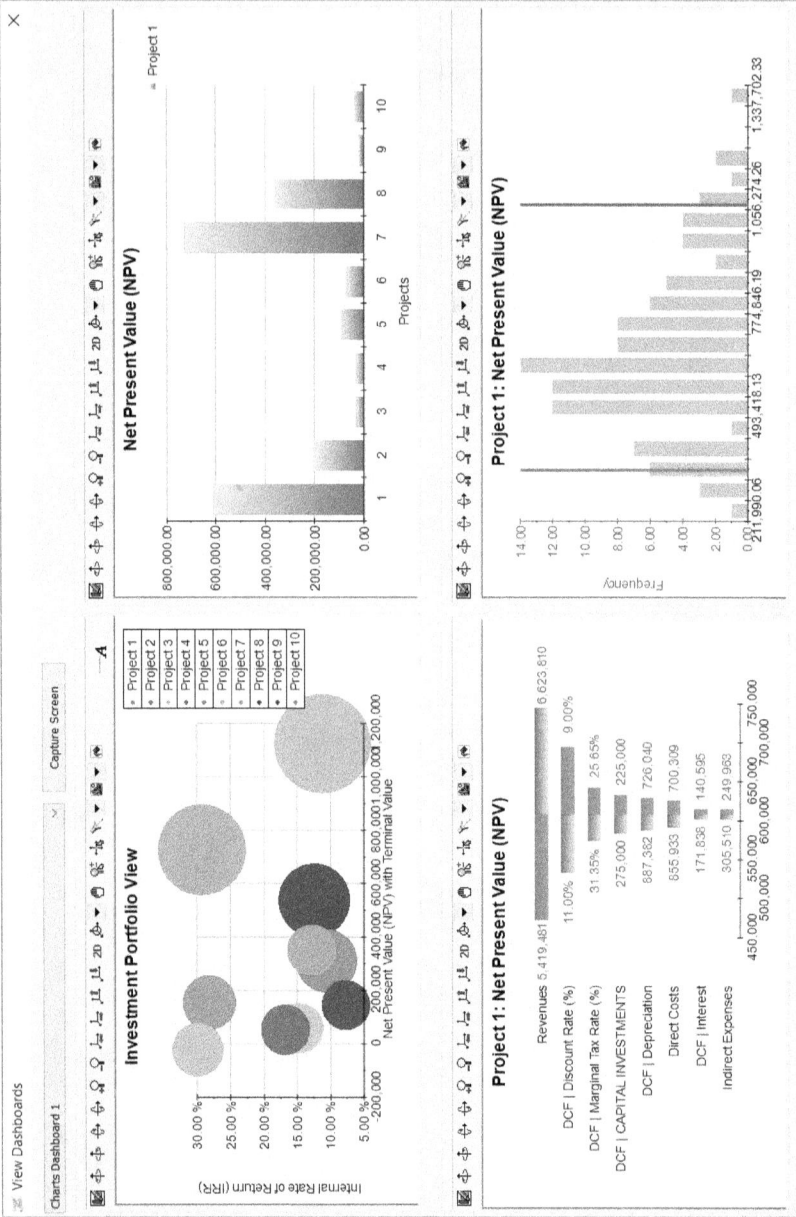

Figure 9.5 – Management Dashboards (1)

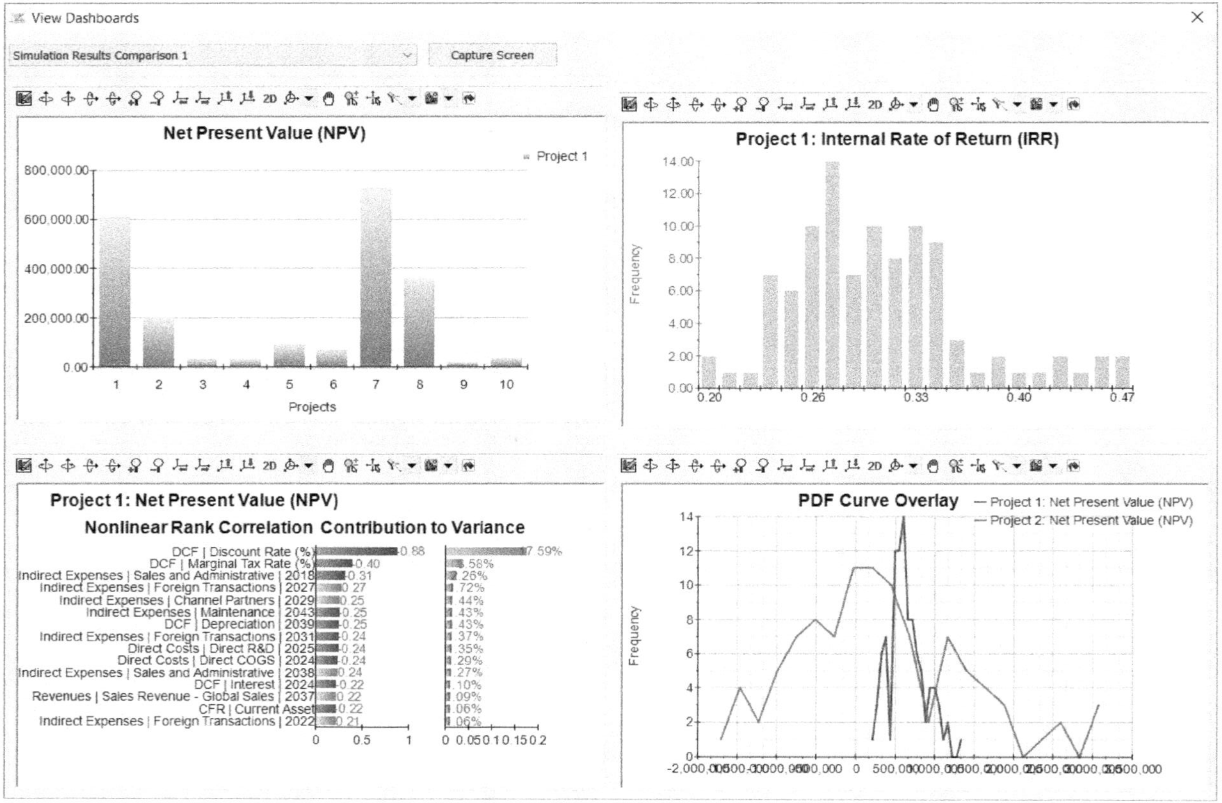

Figure 9.6 – Management Dashboards (2)

≚ [EXAMPLE] - PROJECT ECONOMICS ANALYSIS TOOL — ☐ ✕

File Edit Projects Report Tools Language Decimals Help

Welcome to the ROV Project Economics Analysis Tool (PEAT). This module will help you set up a series of projects or Capital Investment Options, model their Cash Flows, Simulate Risks, and run Advanced Analytics; perform Forecasting and Prediction Modeling; and Optimize your Investment Portfolio subject to Budgetary and other Constraints.

Discounted Cash Flow   Applied Analytics   Risk Simulation   Options Valuation   Forecast Prediction   Portfolio Optimization   Dashboard   Knowledge Center

Step-by-Step Procedures   Practical Applications   Getting Started Videos

| << Prev | Step 03 of 28 | Next >> |

Custom Calculation tab is also available for making your own custom calculations just as you would in an Excel spreadsheet. Clicking on the FUNCTION F(X) button will provide you with a list of the supported functions you can use in this tab. Other basic mathematical functions are also supported, such as +, −, /, *, ^. If you use this optional Custom Calculation tab and wish to link some cells to the input tabs (e.g., Option 1), you can select the cells, right-click, and select LINK TO. Then proceed to the location in the Option tabs and highlight the location of the input cells you wish to link to, right-click, and select LINK FROM. Any subsequent changes you make in the Custom Calculations tab will be updated in the linked input assumption cells.

PEO Standard Economic   Applied Analytics   Risk Simulation   Option 1   Option 2   Option 3   Option 4   Option 5   Option 6   Option 7   Option 8   Option 9   Option 10   Portfolio Analysis

Global Settings   Custom 1   Options Valuation   Forecast Prediction   Portfolio Optimization   Dashboard   Knowledge Center

Use this custom calculations sheet to perform your own intermediate computations that will be saved with the current file that can also be linked to the input sheets (simply select the cells you wish to create a live link, right-click and select LINK TO... then in the input worksheets, select the relevant input cells, right-click and select LINK FROM... and choose the relevant inputs to use). Alternatively, select the cells you wish, right-click COPY and paste the contents into the relevant input tabs (e.g., Option 1), you can select the cells, right-click, and select LINK TO. The main functions supported include: +, −, /, *, ^, ABS, LN, LOG, POWER, SUM, AVERAGE, MIN, MAX. A simple copy/paste from Excel will only paste the model's values, versus first changing to Formula View (CTRL + ~ in Excel, i.e., control slide) and then copy/paste will bring over the Excel functions and computations as well. When pasting complex models in Formula View, we recommend temporarily turning off Auto Calculate.

☑ Auto Calculate   Calculate   Grid...   Full Grid   Excel...   Refresh Links

f(x) >>	=AVERAGE(B3:P6)															
	A	B	C		I	J	K	L	M	N	O	P
1		2010	2011		2017	2018	2019	2020	2021	2022	2023	2024
2		8.56	9.04		9.31	9.30	10.44	9.99	10.49	11.55	12.81	12.18
3		7.41	9.23		10.24	9.79	10.37	11.13	11.40	11.55	11.98	13.34
4		9.02	9.07		9.06	10.31	11.26	10.58	11.25	11.22	11.66	13.88
5		8.79	7.90		10.22	10.79	10.02	10.30	11.40	10.67	11.74	12.06
6		8.66	8.30		10.14	10.15	10.18	10.38	10.42	10.75	12.56	12.75
7												
8		8.532	8.708		9.794	10.068	10.454	10.476	10.992	11.148	12.15	12.842
9												
10												
11												

Functions

Function
ABS(Value)
AVERAGE(ARRAY)
CONCATENATE(String1, [String2], ...)
LEFT(String, Num)
LEN(String)
LN(Value)
LOG(X, Base)
LOG10(Value)
MAX(ARRAY)
MIN(ARRAY)
POWER(X, Y)
RIGHT(String, Num)
ROUND(Value, Num)
SUM(ARRAY)

Figure 9.7 – Knowledge Center: Step-by-Step Procedures

Welcome to the ROV Project Economics Analysis Tool (PEAT). This module will help you set up a series of projects or Capital Investment Options, model their Cash Flows, Simulate Risks, and run Advanced Analytics; perform Forecasting and Prediction Modeling; and Optimize your Investment Portfolio subject to Budgetary and other Constraints.

Discounted Cash Flow   Applied Analytics   Risk Simulation   Options Strategies   Options Valuation   Forecast Prediction   Portfolio Optimization   Dashboard   Knowledge Center

Step-by-Step Procedures   Practical Applications   Getting Started Videos

<< Prev   Lesson 20 of 20   Next >>

Lesson 20. The S-Curves for the distribution (green curve) can be used to arrive at the same conclusions... The 50th percentile is on the left of the other two curves (indicating a lower median or central tendency), the width from minimum to maximum is the widest (indicating a higher standard deviation or risk spread), the area above the 45 degree line is greater than the area below (indicating a positive skew), and the right tail is longer than the other two distributions, indicating a higher kurtosis.

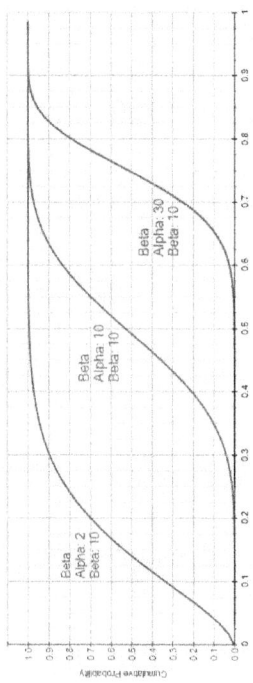

Figure 9.8 – Knowledge Center: Basic Project Economic Lessons

[EXAMPLE] - PROJECT ECONOMICS ANALYSIS TOOL

File   Edit   Projects   Report   Tools   Language   Decimals   Help

Welcome to the ROV Project Economics Analysis Tool (PEAT). This module will help you set up a series of projects or Capital Investment Options, model their Cash Flows, Simulate Risks, and run Advanced Analytics; perform Forecasting and Prediction Modeling; and Optimize your Investment Portfolio subject to Budgetary and other Constraints.

Discounted Cash Flow   Applied Analytics   Risk Simulation   Options Strategies   Options Valuation   Forecast Prediction   Portfolio Optimization   Dashboard   Knowledge Center

Step-by-Step Procedures   Practical Applications   Getting Started Videos

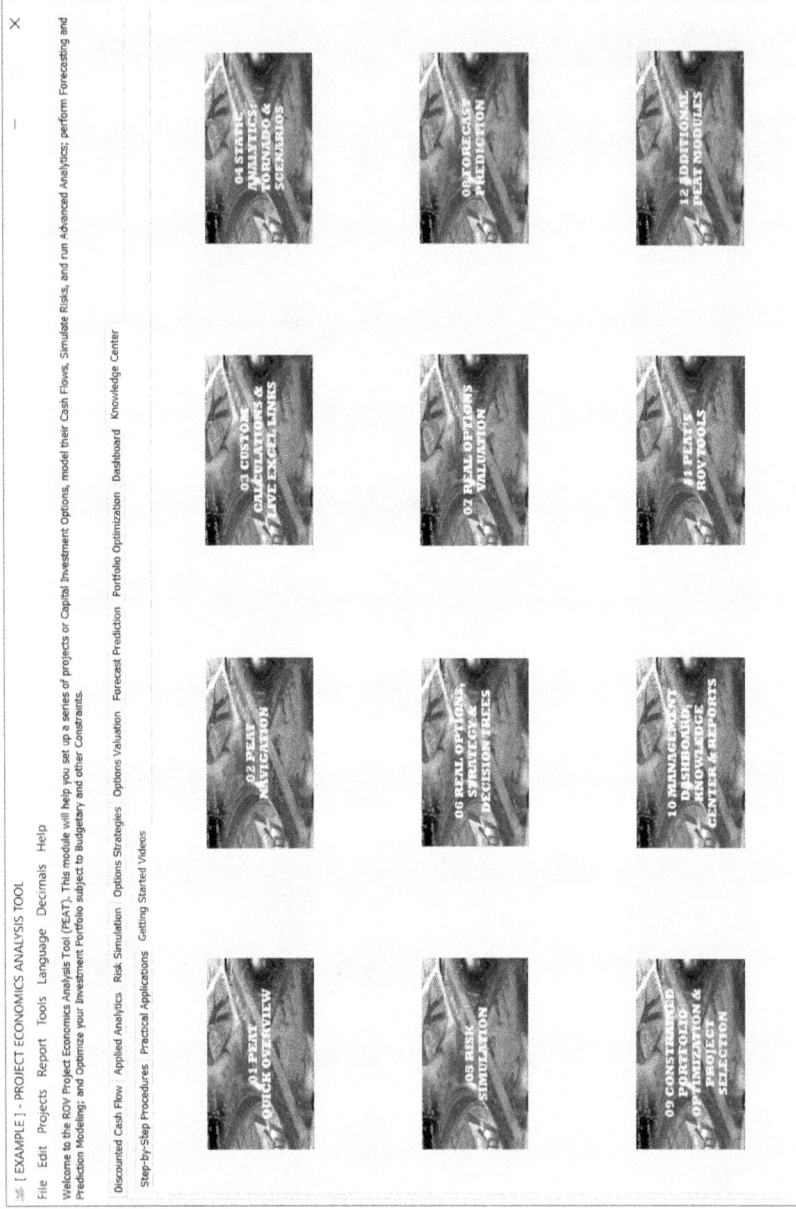

01 PEAT QUICK OVERVIEW

02 PEAT NAVIGATION

03 CUSTOM CALCULATIONS & LIVE EXCEL LINKS

04 STATIC ANALYTICS, TORNADO & SCENARIOS

05 RISK SIMULATION

06 REAL OPTIONS STRATEGY & DECISION TREES

07 REAL OPTIONS VALUATION

08 FORECAST PREDICTION

09 CONSTRAINED PORTFOLIO OPTIMIZATION & PROJECT SELECTION

10 MANAGEMENT DASHBOARD, KNOWLEDGE CENTER & REPORTS

11 PEAT ROV TOOLS

12 ADDITIONAL PEAT MODULES

Figure 9.9 – Knowledge Center: Getting Started Videos

FORMULAE SUMMARY

The following lists some of the basic equations used in the static models (i.e., they do not include simulation, forecasting, optimization, or real options models) of this DCF module in PEAT.

Project or Company Value:

$$\frac{FCF_1}{(1+WACC)^1} + \frac{FCF_2}{(1+WACC)^2} + \ldots + \frac{FCF_N}{(1+WACC)^N} = \sum_{t=0}^{N} \frac{FCF_t}{(1+WACC)^t}$$

Future Value:

Discrete: $FV_n = PV_0(1+i)^n = PV_0[FVIF_{i,n}]$

Continuous: $FV_n = PV_0 e^{in}$

Present Value:

Discrete: $PV_0 = \frac{FV_n}{(1+i)^n} = FV_n\left[\frac{1}{1+i}\right]^n = FV_n[PVIF_{i,n}]$

Continuous: $PV_0 = FV_n e^{-in}$

Future Value of an Annuity:

$$FVA_n = PMT[\sum_{t=1}^{n}(1+i)^{n-t}] = PMT\left[\frac{(1+i)^n}{i} - \frac{1}{i}\right] = PMT[FVIFA_{i,n}]$$

Present Value of an Annuity:

$$PVA_0 = \sum_{t=1}^{n}\frac{PMT}{(1+i)^t} = PMT\left(\frac{1}{i} - \frac{1}{i(1+i)^n}\right) = PMT[PVIFA_{i,n}]$$

Future Value of an Annuity Due:

$$FVA_n = PMT[\sum_{t=1}^{n}(1+i)^{n-t}](1+i) = PMT\left[\frac{(1+i)^n}{i} - \frac{1}{i}\right](1+i) =$$

$$PMT[FVIFA_{i,n}](1+i)$$

Present Value of an Annuity Due:

$$PVA_0 = \left[\sum_{t=1}^{n} \frac{PMT}{(1+i)^t}\right](1+i) = PMT\left(\frac{1}{i} - \frac{1}{i(1+i)^n}\right)(1+i) =$$

$$PMT[PVIFA_{i,n}](1+i)$$

Present Value of Perpetuity:

$$PV_0 = \frac{PMT}{i}$$

Sum of Present Values of Uneven Cash Flows:

$$\sum PV_0 = \sum_{t=1}^{n} CF_t \left[\frac{1}{1+i}\right]^t = \sum_{t=1}^{n} CF_t \left[PVIF_{i,t}\right]$$

Multiple Compounding Periods Adjustment to N and i:

$$n \times p \text{ and } i \div p$$

Effective Annual Rate:

$$EAR = \left[1 + \frac{i}{p}\right]^p - 1$$

Net Present Value:

$$NPV = CF_0 + \frac{CF_1}{(1+k)^1} + \frac{CF_2}{(1+k)^2} + \ldots + \frac{CF_N}{(1+k)^N} = \sum_{t=0}^{N} \frac{CF_t}{(1+k)^t}$$

Internal Rate of Return:

$$NPV = \sum_{t=0}^{N} \frac{CF_t}{(1+IRR)^t} = 0$$

Modified IRR (MIRR):

$$\sum_{t=0}^{N} \frac{COF_t}{(1+WACC)^t} = \sum_{t=0}^{N} \frac{CIF_t(1+WACC)^{N-t}}{(1+MIRR)^N}$$

Weighted Average Cost of Capital:

$$WACC = \omega_d k_d (1-\tau) + \omega_p k_p + \omega_e k_e$$

Profitability Index and Return on Investment:

$$\frac{\sum_{t=1}^{N}\frac{CF_t}{(1+WACC)^t}}{CF_0} = \frac{PV\ Cash\ Flows}{Initial\ Cost}$$

$$ROI = PI - 1 = \frac{\sum_{t=1}^{N}\frac{CF_t}{(1+WACC)^t}-CF_0}{CF_0} = \frac{Benefit-Cost}{Cost}$$

Cost of Debt:

$$k_d - \tau k_d = k_d(1-\tau)$$

Cost of Preferred Stock:

$$k_p = \frac{D_p}{P_{net}}$$

Cost of Common Equity (Capital Asset Pricing Model):

$$k_s = k_{rf} + \beta_i(k_m - k_{rf})$$

Cost of Common Equity (Discounted Cash Flow Model):

$$k_e = \frac{D_0(1+g)}{P_0(1-F)} + g = \frac{D_1}{P_{net}} + g \quad and\ k_s = \frac{D_0(1+g)}{P_0} + g$$

Cost of Common Equity (Bond Yield):

$$k_s = Bond\ Yield + Risk\ Premium$$

Market Risk Premium:

$$MRP = k_m - k_{rf}$$

Growth Rate:

$$g = ROE(1-Payout) = ROE(Retention\ Rate)$$

Securities Market Line:

$$E[R_i] = R_{rf} + (E[R_m] - R_{rf})\frac{\rho_{i,m}\sigma_i\sigma_m}{\sigma_m^2} = R_{rf} + (E[R_m] - R_{rf})\frac{cov_{i,m}}{var_m}$$

Bond Valuation:

$$V_B = \sum_{i=1}^{n} \frac{I}{(1+k_d)^t} + \frac{M}{(1+k_d)^N} = I\left(\frac{1}{k_d} - \frac{1}{k_d(1+k_d)^N}\right) + \frac{M}{(1+k_d)^N}$$

Stock Valuation:

$$\hat{P}_0 = \frac{D_1}{(1+k_S)^1} + \frac{D_1}{(1+k_S)^2} + \ldots + \frac{D_1}{(1+k_S)^\infty} = \sum_{t=1}^{\infty} \frac{D_t}{(1+k_S)^t}$$

Earnings Before Interest, Taxes, Depreciation, and Amortization (EBITDA):

Revenue – Operating Expenses

Earnings Before Interest and Taxes (EBIT) or Operating Income:

EBITDA – Depreciation – Amortization

Net Operating Profit After Taxes (NOPAT) and Net Income (NI):

NOPAT = EBIT (1 – Tax Rate) and

NI = (EBIT – Interest)(1 – Tax)

Net Cash Flow (NCF):

Net Income + Depreciation + Amortization

Operating Cash Flow – (Interest Charges)(1 – Tax Rate)

Operating Cash Flow (OCF):

(EBIT)(1 – Tax Rate) + Depreciation + Amortization

NOPAT + Depreciation + Amortization

Net Operating Working Capital (NOWC):

Current Assets – Current Liabilities

Current Assets:

Cash + Accounts Receivables + Inventories

Current Liabilities:

Accounts Payable + Accruals + Wages Payable

Net Operating Capital:

NOWC + Operating Long-Term Assets

Free Cash Flow (FCF):

NOPAT – Net Investment in Operating Capital

Operating Cash Flow – Gross Investment in Operating Capital

Return on Invested Capital (ROIC):

NOPAT ÷ Total Net Operating Capital

Net Investment in Operating Capital:

Change in Net Operating Capital Year Over Year

Gross Investment in Operating Capital:

Net Investment in Operating Capital + Depreciation + Amortization

Market Value Added (MVA):

Market Value of Stock – Equity Capital Supplied

(Shares Outstanding) (Stock Price) – Common Equity

MV Stock + MV Debt – Investor Supplied Capital

Economic Value Added (EVA):

NOPAT – After-Tax Cost of Capital

EBIT(1 –Tax Rate) – (Total Net Operating Capital)(WACC)

Total Net Operating Capital (ROIC – WACC)

Common Stockholders' Equity (Net Worth):

Assets – Liabilities – Preferred Stock

Earnings Per Share (EPS):

Net Income ÷ Common Shares Outstanding

Dividends Per Share (DPS):

Dividends ÷ Common Shares Outstanding

Book Value Per Share (BV):

Total Common Equity ÷ Common Shares Outstanding

Equivalent Pre-Tax Yield on Taxable Bond:

(Yield on Nontaxable Bond) ÷ (1 – Marginal Tax Rate)

Equivalent Yield on Nontaxable Bond:

(Pre-Tax Yield on Taxable Bond)(1 – Marginal Tax Rate)

After Tax Income:

(Before Tax Income)(1 – Effective Tax Rate)

Current Ratio (CR):

Current Assets ÷ Current Liabilities

Quick or Acid Test (QR):

(Current Assets – Inventories) ÷ Current Liabilities

Inventory Turnover (IT):

Sales ÷ Inventory

Days Sales Outstanding (DSO):

Receivables ÷ (Annual Sales/360) or Receivables ÷ Average Sales Per Day

Fixed Assets Turnover (FAT):

Sales ÷ Net Fixed Assets

Total Assets Turnover (TAT):

Sales ÷ Total Assets

Total Debt to Total Assets (DA):

Total Debt ÷ Total Assets

Times Interest Earned (TIE):

Earnings Before Interest and Taxes (EBIT) ÷ Interest Charge

Profit Margin on Sales (PM):

Net Income Available to Stockholders ÷ Sales

Basic Earning Power (BEP):

Earnings Before Interest and Taxes (EBIT) ÷ Total Assets

Price/Earnings (PE):

Price Per Share ÷ Earnings Per Share

Market to Book (MB):

Market Price Per Share ÷ Book Value Per Share

Equity Multiplier (EM):

Total Asset ÷ Total Equity

Debt Equity (DE):

Total Debt ÷ Total Equity

Debt Ratio (DR):

Total Debt ÷ Total Assets = 1 – (1 ÷ Equity Multiplier)

Operating Profitability:

NOPAT ÷ Sales

Capital Requirements:

Operating Capital ÷ Sales

Return on Asset (ROA):

Net Income Available to Stockholders ÷ Total Assets

(Net Income ÷ Sales) × (Sales ÷ Total Assets) = Profit Margin x TAT

Return on Common Equity (ROE):

Net Income Available to Stockholders ÷ Common Equity

ROA x Equity Multiplier

(Net Income ÷ Total Assets) × (Total Assets ÷ Common Equity)

Profit Margin x Total Asset Turnover × Equity Multiplier

(Net Income ÷ Sales) × (Sales ÷ Assets) × (Assets ÷ Equity)

$$ROE = \frac{NI}{CE} = \frac{NI}{CE} \times \frac{S}{S} \times \frac{TA}{TA} = \frac{NI}{S} \times \frac{TA}{CE} \times \frac{S}{TA} = \frac{TA}{CE} \times \frac{NI}{TA}$$

SOFTWARE DOWNLOAD & INSTALL

As current versions of the software are continually updated, we highly recommend that you visit the Real Options Valuation, Inc., website and follow the instructions below to install the latest software applications.

- **Step 1**: Visit **www.realoptionsvaluation.com** and click on **Downloads** and **Download Software** (Figure A). You will be prompted to log in. Please first register if you are a first-time user (Figure B) and an automated e-mail will be sent to you within several minutes. (If you do not receive a registration e-mail after you register, then please send a note to support@realoptionsvaluation.com.) While waiting for the automated e-mail, browse this page and see the free getting started videos, case studies, and sample models you can download.

- **Step 2**: Return to this site and LOGIN using the login credentials you received via e-mail. Download and install the latest versions of **Risk Simulator** and **Real Options SLS** on this Web page. The download links, installation instructions, and Hardware ID information are also presented on this page (Figure C).

- **Step 3**: After installing the software, start Excel and you will see a Risk Simulator ribbon. Follow the instructions provided on the Web page to obtain and e-mail support@realoptionsvaluation.com your Hardware ID and mention the code "**MR3E 30 Days**" and you will be sent a free extended 30-day license to use both the Risk Simulator and Real Options SLS software.

Real Options Valuation

Testimonials | FAQ | Global Partners | Contact Us

🇬🇧 English   🇨🇳 Chinese (Simplified)   🇹🇼 Chinese (Traditional)   🇫🇷 French   🇩🇪 German   🇮🇹 Italian
🇯🇵 Japanese   🇰🇷 Korean   🇧🇷 Portuguese (Brazil)   🇷🇺 Russian   🇪🇸 Spanish

0 items · $0.00

CQRM CERTIFICATE | TRAINING | CONSULTING | SOFTWARE | BOOKS | DOWNLOADS | PURCHASE |

SOFTWARE DOWNLOADS

GETTING STARTED AND
MODELING VIDEOS

PRODUCT BROCHURES

SAMPLE MODELS

WHITEPAPERS AND CASE STUDIES

DOWNLOAD CENTER

You can also visit our mirror download site if you have problems downloading from this page

Welcome to Real Options Valuation, Inc.'s download center. Here you will be able to download purchased (license information required to install these full versions), product brochures, case started in using our software, as well as sample Excel models to use with Risk Simulator and Re... versions of the software you have ...ple training videos to help you get ...ftware.

GETTING STARTED AND MODELING VIDEOS

The following are some live-motion and voice narrated videos which are playable on your computer using Windows Media Player or other video players capable of WMV playback. You can simply click on any of these links below to view the streaming videos.

ROV SOFTWARE GETTING STARTED VIDEOS

We also have some more detailed Risk Analysis and Risk Simulator software getting started videos that you can download and watch. These videos total about 2 hours. For even more detailed training, please check out our set of 12 Training DVDs (over 30 hours) or our hands-on Certified in Risk Management seminars (4 days). The following are updated detailed getting started videos on Risk Simulator, featuring all the new tools such as Auto ARIMA, GARCH, JS Curves, Cubic Spline, Maximum Likelihood, Data Diagnostics, Statistical Analysis, Modeling Toolkit, and more...

Figure A: Step 1 – Software download site

DOWNLOAD CENTER

You can also visit our mirror download site if you have problems downloading from this page

Welcome to Real Options Valuation, Inc.'s download center. Here you will be able to download trial versions of our software, full versions of the software you have purchased (license information required to install these full versions), product brochures, case studies and white papers, and sample training videos to help you get started in using our software, as well as sample Excel models to use with Risk Simulator and Real Options Super Lattice Solver software.

YOU ARE REQUIRED TO LOGIN TO VIEW THIS PAGE.

Username

Password

LOG IN   REGISTER

Figure B: Register if you are a first-time visitor

English | Chinese (Simplified) | Chinese (Traditional) | French | German | Italian
Japanese | Korean | Portuguese (Brazil) | Russian | Spanish

0 more $0.00

CQRM CERTIFICATE | TRAINING | CONSULTING | SOFTWARE | BOOKS | DOWNLOADS | PURCHASE |

FULL & TRIAL VERSION DOWNLOAD:

Download Risk Simulator 2018 – Auto Installer
Download Risk Simulator 2018 – Auto Installer (mirror site)
Download Risk Simulator 2018 – For 32 Bit Excel
Download Risk Simulator 2018 – For 32 Bit Excel (mirror site)
Download Risk Simulator 2018 – For 64 Bit Excel
Download Risk Simulator 2018 – For 64 Bit Excel (mirror site)

Download OLDER version of Risk Simulator 2014 [WIN x64 and Excel x32 edition]
Download OLDER version of Risk Simulator 2014 [WIN x64 and Excel x32 edition] (mirror site)

This is a full version of the software but will expire in 15 days, during which time you can purchase a license to permanently unlock the software. Please first uninstall all previous versions of Risk Simulator before installing this newer version.

To permanently unlock the software, purchase a license and e-mail us your Hardware ID (after installing the software, start Excel, click on Risk Simulator License, and e-mail admin@realoptionsvaluation.com the 16 to 20 digit Hardware ID located on the bottom left of the splash screen). We will then e-mail you a permanent license file. Save this file to your hard drive, start Excel, click on Risk Simulator License, Install License and point to the location of this license file, restart Excel and you are now permanently licensed. Installing the license only takes a few seconds.

SYSTEM REQUIREMENTS, FAQ, AND ADDITIONAL RESOURCES:

* Windows 7, 8, and 10 (32 and 64 bits)
* Microsoft Excel 2010, 2013, or 2016
* 2GB RAM Minimum (4 GB recommended)
* 600 MB Hard Drive
* Administrative Rights to install software
* Microsoft .NET Framework 2.0, 3.0, 3.5 or later
* MAC OS users will require either Virtual Machine or Parallels running Microsoft Excel

Figure C: Download links and hardware ID instructions

INDEX